OPPOSING
VIEWPOINTS®
SERIES

D0042711

The Film Industry

Other Books of Related Interest:

Opposing Viewpoints Series
Copyright Infringement

At Issue Series
Can Celebrities Change the World?

Current Controversies Series
Media Ethics

"Congress shall make no law . . . abridging the freedom of speech, or of the press."

First Amendment to the U.S. Constitution

The basic foundation of our democracy is the First Amendment guarantee of freedom of expression. The Opposing Viewpoints Series is dedicated to the concept of this basic freedom and the idea that it is more important to practice it than to enshrine it.

OPPOSING
VIEWPOINTS®
SERIES

The Film Industry

Roman Espejo, Book Editor

GREENHAVEN PRESS
A part of Gale, Cengage Learning

GALE
CENGAGE Learning·

Detroit • New York • San Francisco • New Haven, Conn • Waterville, Maine • London

GALE
CENGAGE Learning™

Christine Nasso, *Publisher*
Elizabeth Des Chenes, *Managing Editor*

© 2009 Greenhaven Press, a part of Gale, Cengage Learning.

Gale and Greenhaven Press are registered trademarks used herein under license.

For more information, contact:
Greenhaven Press
27500 Drake Rd.
Farmington Hills, MI 48331-3535
Or you can visit our Internet site at gale.cengage.com

For product information and technology assistance, contact us at

Gale Customer Support, 1-800-877-4253
For permission to use material from this text or product, submit all requests online at
www.cengage.com/permissions

Further permissions questions can be emailed to permissionrequest@cengage.com

Articles in Greenhaven Press anthologies are often edited for length to meet page requirements. In addition, original titles of these works are changed to clearly present the main thesis and to explicitly indicate the author's opinion. Every effort is made to ensure that Greenhaven Press accurately reflects the original intent of the authors. Every effort has been made to trace the owners of copyrighted material.

Cover photograph reproduced by Stockbyte/Getty Images.

LIBRARY OF CONGRESS CATALOGING-IN-PUBLICATION DATA

The film industry / Roman Espejo, book editor.
   p. cm. -- (Opposing viewpoints)
   Includes bibliographical references and index.
   ISBN 978-0-7377-4364-7 (hardcover)
   ISBN 978-0-7377-4363-0 (pbk.)
   1. Motion picture industry--United States--History--21st century. 2. Motion pictures--Social aspects--United States. 3. Motion pictures--Censorship--United States. I. Espejo, Roman, 1977-
   PN1993.5.U6F495 2009
   384'.80973--dc22
                                                        2009002457

Printed in the United States of America
1 2 3 4 5 6 7 13 12 11 10 09

Contents

Chapter 2: Are Film Ratings Effective?

Chapter 3: Is the Film Industry Appropriately Regulated?

Chapter 4: What Is the Future of the Film Industry?

Why Consider Opposing Viewpoints?

> *"The only way in which a human being can make some approach to knowing the whole of a subject is by hearing what can be said about it by persons of every variety of opinion and studying all modes in which it can be looked at by every character of mind. No wise man ever acquired his wisdom in any mode but this."*
>
> *John Stuart Mill*

In our media-intensive culture it is not difficult to find differing opinions. Thousands of newspapers and magazines and dozens of radio and television talk shows resound with differing points of view. The difficulty lies in deciding which opinion to agree with and which "experts" seem the most credible. The more inundated we become with differing opinions and claims, the more essential it is to hone critical reading and thinking skills to evaluate these ideas. Opposing Viewpoints books address this problem directly by presenting stimulating debates that can be used to enhance and teach these skills. The varied opinions contained in each book examine many different aspects of a single issue. While examining these conveniently edited opposing views, readers can develop critical thinking skills such as the ability to compare and contrast authors' credibility, facts, argumentation styles, use of persuasive techniques, and other stylistic tools. In short, the Opposing Viewpoints Series is an ideal way to attain the higher-level thinking and reading skills so essential in a culture of diverse and contradictory opinions.

In addition to providing a tool for critical thinking, Opposing Viewpoints books challenge readers to question their own strongly held opinions and assumptions. Most people form their opinions on the basis of upbringing, peer pressure, and personal, cultural, or professional bias. By reading carefully balanced opposing views, readers must directly confront new ideas as well as the opinions of those with whom they disagree. This is not to simplistically argue that everyone who reads opposing views will—or should—change his or her opinion. Instead, the series enhances readers' understanding of their own views by encouraging confrontation with opposing ideas. Careful examination of others' views can lead to the readers' understanding of the logical inconsistencies in their own opinions, perspective on why they hold an opinion, and the consideration of the possibility that their opinion requires further evaluation.

Evaluating Other Opinions

To ensure that this type of examination occurs, Opposing Viewpoints books present all types of opinions. Prominent spokespeople on different sides of each issue as well as well-known professionals from many disciplines challenge the reader. An additional goal of the series is to provide a forum for other, less known, or even unpopular viewpoints. The opinion of an ordinary person who has had to make the decision to cut off life support from a terminally ill relative, for example, may be just as valuable and provide just as much insight as a medical ethicist's professional opinion. The editors have two additional purposes in including these less known views. One, the editors encourage readers to respect others' opinions—even when not enhanced by professional credibility. It is only by reading or listening to and objectively evaluating others' ideas that one can determine whether they are worthy of consideration. Two, the inclusion of such viewpoints encourages the important critical thinking skill of objectively evaluating an author's credentials and bias. This evaluation will illuminate an author's reasons for taking a particular stance on an issue and will aid in readers' evaluation of the author's ideas.

It is our hope that these books will give readers a deeper understanding of the issues debated and an appreciation of the complexity of even seemingly simple issues when good and honest people disagree. This awareness is particularly important in a democratic society such as ours in which people enter into public debate to determine the common good. Those with whom one disagrees should not be regarded as enemies but rather as people whose views deserve careful examination and may shed light on one's own.

Thomas Jefferson once said that "difference of opinion leads to inquiry, and inquiry to truth." Jefferson, a broadly educated man, argued that "if a nation expects to be ignorant and free . . . it expects what never was and never will be." As individuals and as a nation, it is imperative that we consider the opinions of others and examine them with skill and discernment. The Opposing Viewpoints Series is intended to help readers achieve this goal.

David L. Bender and Bruno Leone,
Founders

Introduction

"Hollywood laid much of the blame for illegal movie downloading on college students. Now, it says its math was wrong."

—*Associated Press*

In January 2008, Seth Oster, executive vice president of corporate communications for the Motion Picture Association of America (MPAA), released a statement retracting a claim that the trade association made three years earlier, which was based on a movie piracy study conducted by consulting firm LEK. The MPAA had reported that American colleges and universities were accountable for 44 percent of the film industry's annual domestic losses of $6.1 billion. "The 2007 study will report that number to be approximately 15 percent—or nearly a quarter of a billion dollars in stolen content annually by college students in the U.S.," Oster stated. However, he maintained that college students are still a major part of Hollywood's piracy dilemma. "The latest data confirms that college campuses are still faced with a significant problem. Although college students make up 3 percent of the population, they are responsible for a disproportionate amount of stolen movie products in this country."

Critics of the MPAA expressed outrage at this admission, alleging that the association used an exaggerated claim and dubious research to influence public policy, including the College Opportunity and Affordability Act of 2008. (Signed into law by former president George W. Bush in August 2008, it requires schools to use Internet filters to deter file sharing.) Nate Anderson, senior editor of technology at news site ArsTechnica, argues, "[T]he MPAA lobbying drive to turn universities into copyright cops touches a raw nerve. The fact that one of the key data points in this lobbying for the last two years was overstated by a factor of three is bad. . . ." Others accuse the trade association of crying wolf on campus piracy because box-office attendance is booming. Hugh D'Andrade of the Electronic Frontier Foundation contends that "the film industry is enjoying record year after record year," raking in $9.3 billion in 2007, a 5 percent jump from the previous year.

Still, the MPAA asserts that academic institutions stand to benefit, in several ways, from ramping up their anti-piracy efforts. Chairman Dan Glickman proposes that responding to file-sharing lawsuits and infringement notices from copyright holders is costly and creates undue burdens for university and college administrators. Furthermore, he insists that illegal movie downloading on peer-to-peer (P2P) services consumes bandwidth reserved for educational purposes as well as exposes school networks and computers to viruses, spyware, and other malware. "Addressing these issues," Glickman says, "can have tremendous positive effects on the operation and cost efficiencies of the university network." He cites the University of Florida's CGRID program as a successful model, which reportedly reduced attempts of illegal file sharing by 80 percent in just a few years, saving the university $2 million by freeing its networks from bandwidth-hungry P2P services.

Nonetheless, according to some analysts, fighting movie piracy in colleges and universities is expensive in itself. According to "The Campus Costs of P2P Compliance," a 2008 study conducted by the Campus Computing Project, private universities spent an average of $408,000 to deal with illegal file sharing during the 2007 academic year, while public schools spent about $170,000 each. Kenneth C. Green, the project's founding director, contends that such anti-piracy measures have university staff throughout the country performing "pro bono enforcement for the entertainment industry." He also upholds that the passing of the College Opportunity and Affordability Act places academic institutions under additional financial strain. "In many cases, colleges and universities had little or no money in their budgets [in 2008] for either notification systems or P2P monitoring technology."

The MPAA's battle against piracy, however, will not let up in the near future. In his own words, Glickman declares, "Piracy is the greatest obstacle the film industry currently faces." And as a phenomenally popular form of entertainment, films bring other issues into focus, such as media violence, censorship, and technology. In *Opposing Viewpoints: The Film Industry*, these topics and more are examined in the following chapters: How Does the Film Industry Affect Society? Are Film Ratings Effective? Is the Film Industry Appropriately Regulated? What Is the Future of the Film Industry? The authors—movie critics, industry insiders, and media experts—offer their views and insights on the motion picture as an art form, as a business, and as a part of culture.

OPPOSING
VIEWPOINTS®
SERIES

CHAPTER 1

How Does the Film Industry Affect Society?

Chapter Preface

The 2007 Virginia Tech shootings placed violence in the media, particularly in movies, under renewed scrutiny. Seung-Hui Cho, the lone gunman and an English major at the university, sent a media kit to NBC's Manhattan headquarters containing photos of himself posing with various weapons. Upon the release of the photos, Virginia Tech film instructor Paul Harrill alleged that some of Cho's photos resembled scenes from 2003's *Oldboy*, a critically acclaimed revenge thriller from South Korea—fueling speculation that life had, horrifically, imitated art.

Investigators could not determine a connection between Cho and *Oldboy*, and Harrill downplayed his claim as an "observation." But the storm surrounding film violence—especially its potential effects on youths—did not subside. In reaction to the Virginia Tech shootings and glowing reviews of *Oldboy*, entertainment journalist Nikki Finke argued, "I just don't understand how critics with even a shred of humanity keep supporting films that celebrate violence in all its awfulness." Under pressure, the film industry also checked itself. For instance, an American adaptation of Japanese cult favorite *Battle Royale*, in which island-marooned junior high classmates are ordered to kill each other, faces uncertainty. When asked about the project's future, producer Roy Lee stated, "[W]e might be a little more sensitive to some of the issues."

Other observers, nonetheless, squarely blame the accessibility of firearms for real-life eruptions of lethal violence. Richard Corliss, a senior writer for *Time*, asserts, "If you're looking for the villain behind Cho's sadistic spree, consider what it has in common with every multiple-murder tragedy in recent U.S. history: the young man had easy access to a few of the 200 million guns available in this country, and used them to slaughter people who never did him harm." And some industry professionals maintain that bloodshed on the silver screen should not be taken at face value. Years before the tragedy at Virginia Tech, *Oldboy*'s director Park Chan-wook told a magazine, "My films are the stories of people who place the blame for their actions on others because they refuse to take on the blame themselves."

In *Oldboy* and other controversial, graphic movies, directors explore violence, sexuality, and exploitation with an unflinching eye. In the following chapter, authors discuss whether motion pictures are a "mirror to society," or mold society itself.

> *"The world of film . . . need[s] to examine very carefully what happens in our minds when we watch endless violent imagery and feel no wounds or repercussions."*

Movie Violence May Be Harmful

David Thomson

David Thomson is a writer and arts critic. In the following viewpoint, Thomson suggests that cinematic violence may unintentionally harm the minds of its viewers, especially children and adolescents. He states that the thousands of hours of violent imagery in movies that audiences are exposed to—and may not be prepared for—could hinder their ability to connect violence and consequence, resulting in a more dangerous and hostile society. Consequently, in Thomson's view, filmmakers must treat the medium of film as an "engine" of both art and violence, and younger moviegoers must gain a greater understanding of how this engine works.

As you read, consider the following questions:

1. What violent imagery does the author describe in the shower scene from *Psycho?*

2. As stated by the author, how did the very first movie audiences react to cinematic images of an oncoming train?

3. How does the author define an R-rated film?

After a gap of five years, [writer and director] Quentin Tarantino returns to the movies [in 2003] with *Kill Bill,* which is a streamlined version of a kids' video game. It is no surprise that Tarantino should be interested in the spectacle of violence, as *Reservoir Dogs* and *Pulp Fiction* both contained challenging moments of aggression and terror. But they were also pictures about people, and above all people who talked, who gave vent to their feelings and an extraordinary inner life. The pity is, I think, that in reflecting now upon his own talent and his own medium, Tarantino has opted to pursue "pure" cinematic violence and to ignore character and conversation.

A Synonym for Cinema

In many ways, violence is simply a synonym for cinema. People have gone to the movies to see things that have been denied them in real life. Danger, adventure, violence—and success at all three—have always been part of the fantastic experience of sitting in the dark watching the faces of strangers that are as large as the side of a house. And because we at the movies are safe—in the dark, in the warmth, in the company of others—the danger is all the more alluring, and yet all the trickier to handle, because we are not likely to get hurt.

In the *Psycho* shower scene, Alfred Hitchcock filmed the pumping motion of the knife so well that we felt we were being attacked ourselves. People flinched. They shut their eyes. They hid under the seats. They may even have run out of the cinema screaming. But they had lost none of their own blood.

21

The blood, or the chocolate sauce, or whatever Hitchcock used in that quaint black and white film, came from no human being. Not even Janet Leigh or her stand-in was caught up in the slaughter. The character Marion Crane is dead, and however many times you see the film, she dies always at the same point, at the same time, as if it were an appointment she were keeping. But Janet Leigh is alive and well; I saw her in California [in 2002] and interviewed her for this very paper [*The Independent*]. What have audiences ever made of that fascinating confusion? I mean the one in which the character is destroyed so completely that we cannot bear to watch, and yet the actress comes through and can be seen smiling at the Academy Awards. I said that violence in the movies is a tricky business, just as watching any event or situation normally forbidden in life is a very testing sport in fantasy. From the early days in the history of the movies, some people worried that the violence might be infectious, that it might leap out from the screen and claim figures in the audience. When the Lumiere brothers showed their first films in Paris in 1895, one of their subjects was a railway engine drawing slowly into a station. This meant photographing the locomotive as it came towards the camera. Very slowly. But still, some people in that Parisian audience—and Paris has always prided itself on being a very sophisticated city—got up and ran out of the dark because they believed the engine might come out of the screen and hit them.

Is that crazy? Or is it simply the natural fulfillment of all the anticipation and desire that goes into watching movies? A hundred years later, our children, my children, watch another kind of screen, the TV screen, and play computer games on it. They are games of combat. You can stop them playing these games in your house, but then they play them at their friends' houses. They are everywhere. Some people claim that they improve and heighten children's instincts and their ability to solve puzzles. Many people fear that they may give children the notion that violence is a game, and one free from damage or hurt.

A Fatal Notion

In recent years, in Britain and America, children, or people below an age of legal responsibility, have killed other children. In some cases, they killed many children. With guns they found in their parents' rooms. With guns that were so like the guns in video games that they made the same noises and gave the same spurts of fire, and the victim tumbled down in just the same way.

Is this because evil, pure evil, is out and about in the land? Is it because the entire condition in which these children live is itself racked with violence, unhappiness and discontent? Or is it because, in a hundred years, the movies have introduced a fatal notion of separation between violence and consequence? Is that why generals and politicians reporting to us on their victory in Iraq, or wherever, can speak of "collateral damage"—as if those words began to let them think that they were not responsible for the shattering of innocent people?

This is not to propose drastic censorship of violence or of anything in the movies. Is it violent, after all, when a movie cuts from shot A to shot B? We only use the word "cut" because deep down we know that something sharp and severing is happening. A cut is also a joining mechanism, something that brings together an A and a B, so that poetry or beauty or wonder can happen. So that the audience can see, and feel a connection between, hitherto disparate things, which is exactly what we would want art to do.

But the cut is still violent and it holds a quality of intimidation for us: we know that a movie can cut to anything quicker than we can close our eyes, and that is part of the fear and the thrill in being at the movies. Fear and thrill and excitement and being moved; these are all things that we tell

Desensitization to Danger and Violence

Desensitization occurs when an emotional response is repeatedly evoked in situations in which the action tendency that is associated with the emotion proves irrelevant or unnecessary. For example, most people become emotionally aroused when they see a snake slithering toward them. The physiological response they are experiencing is part of what is called the "fight or flight" reaction—an innate tendency that prepares an organism to do what it needs to do when it's threatened. But the individual who spends a good deal of time around harmless, nonpoisonous snakes, knows there is no need to retreat or attack the animal, and over time, the body "learns" not to experience increased heart rates, blood pressure, or other physiological concomitants of fear at the sight of snakes. In a somewhat analogous fashion, exposure to media violence, particularly that which entails bitter hostilities or the graphic display of injuries, initially induces an intense emotional reaction in viewers. Over time and with repeated exposure in the context of entertainment and relaxation, however, many viewers exhibit decreasing emotional responses to the depiction of violence and injury. Studies have documented that desensitization results in reduced arousal and emotional disturbance while witnessing violence. . . .

Joanne Cantor,
"The Psychological Effects of Media Violence on Children and Adolescents," April 19, 2002. http://yourmindonmedia.com.

ourselves we need and want, they are some of the mainsprings of art. And, at its best, we say that film can be an art.

The Real Historical Dangers of Film

But if film, or film on television, is used to show the world the "victory" in Iraq, when what happened was so much more complicated than victory, then the universal importance and power of film may be especially dangerous. [In September 2003], the world at last lost Leni Riefenstahl, who claimed always that she had simply made a documentary record of the Nazi party rallies at Nuremberg. Is that claim accurate? In a way, if you want to know what those rallies looked like, you should go to the films, for their historical value. But it is also true that if you watch *The Triumph of the Will* [Riefenstahl's arguably propagandistic film] for long enough, your foot will start to tap to the pounding beat, the pulse, of the movie. That rhythm is in the drumming, in the marching and in the cutting of the film. It has a power that makes you want to be there, in uniform, as part of the power. That's what propaganda means, and propaganda has not really found a more powerful medium than film.

Leni Riefenstahl was, in effect, banned from making more films by the shock felt after 1945 all around the world—the victorious world—at what Nazism had meant, and at how far the art of film might have been an important instrument in persuading people to join the party, to march with it and to order people into death camps. Should film therefore be censored now? Should it have been censored in the 1930s? Could such censorship have taken effect without military action?

At a more domestic level, what are we to do with our own fascination with violence, except use it like a drug, and let it have its way with us? We could step back and wonder at the larger social and political context in which games of violence can become such an entertainment. In America the ratings system used on films means that children of any age can see R-rated films—the R is for restricted—as long as they are with parents or guardians, or people who will say that they are parents or guardians. This means that an American child of three or four can be taken to see, say *The Silence of the Lambs*, or any other picture which, for good reasons or others, explores violence to the limits of the filmmakers' imagination. I have been in theatres when such children have been crying out loud, and in some cases I have to think that this was because of the fear they felt at what loomed over them. Yet parents told the children, politely or not, to shut up, so that they could continue to enjoy the fantasy. Why is that allowed to happen? Because the film business is so eager to sell every last ticket that it possibly can, that it will let innocent tiny children in to see shows that are simply not fit for them. And, of course, you have to buy a ticket for the child too.

In Their Trigger Fingers

The responsibility of the business and the filmmakers is never satisfied by claims that the public have a right to make their own decisions. People don't always know how "terrible" a film is going to get, or how profound its impact will be. My wife saw *A Clockwork Orange* when she was a teenager and has bad dreams about it still. Stanley Kubrick, an artist by most people's reckoning, made that film in England and then chose to withdraw it because he feared it had been influential in a number of cases of copycat killings in Britain. He was right to make that amendment to his own work—and he only had power over the release of the film in the [United Kingdom] UK—but what are we to say about his decision to make the film in the first place? Was he wrong? Was he misguided? Should we honour his self-censorship? The film is now available again in Britain, after his heirs elected to free it up. Is that the proper respect that an artist deserves? Are we always brave and strong enough to see everything? I don't mean to suggest that film is the source and model of all that is wrong in modern society. But I do think that the world of film, which includes those people who are madly enthusiastic about any film, need to examine very carefully what happens in our minds when we watch endless violent imagery and feel no wounds or repercussions. For one, I am no longer confident that a message has not been passed down to several generations, in their bloodstreams, in their nervous systems and in their trigger fingers.

There is extraordinary violence in society today. It is there in the way we speak to each other and look at each other. Hostile looks, mean words, unkind actions, a steady stream of insults and cheating that are now taken for granted as parts of modern life. We have institutionalised the violence of divorce and broken homes, trusting that our adult emotional needs, our search for happiness, are more important than the damage that is done in break-up. Yet we all know, all of us who have been divorced and have tried again, that there is a damage that is done in these things that does not go away.

Our Everyday Violence

Enough of us know why we are alive. But not enough of us have a sense of purpose that can calm the many contrary tides of aggression that are out there: on the street, in parking battles, in road rage and in that sinister silent metaphor for all kinds of prison camps, the London Tube. Especially the Northern Line, where hideous congestion—people so close to each other they could be having sex—co-exists with a lack of intimacy or shared understanding that is terrifying. Are those passengers waiting for the catastrophic accident that everyone on the Northern Line feels must come? Are they wondering whether, in the event of that, they will behave well, as Londoners did in the Blitz, say, helping each other, being part of a community and a society? But where does this feeling of the crowd and loneliness come from? Does it have anything to do with the very nature of the movies, where the crowd sits in the dark, anonymous and unknown, unrecognised, and watches these huge burnished beautiful faces? Is that a model for religion or fascism? And do we always know how to tell one from the other? So many great films from *Birth of a Nation* to *The Godfather* are crammed with violence, and great directors have always been able to handle the violence so that we feel chastened and purged, changed by it all.

The Engine of Film

But then there is the mass of filmmaking, and it is the mass that really counts, because it is the 20,000 hours of moving imagery that every 18-year-old has seen, in which the brutality of the event and the intimidating aura of the darkness itself, come together in something that is simply and only terrifying and reducing. We are, I fear, so much less than we might be, for reasons that are obvious and over which politicians labour: lack of education, lack of jobs, lack of housing, lack of hope, lack of money.

But is it possible that the movies are the first medium capable of being art, that have in serious ways added to that burden? Do I mean we should stop the movies? No, by no means. You cannot stop a thing after it has been driving at a hundred miles an hour for a hundred years. But we can do so much more to understand it. One step that would make such a difference would be to insist that our children, who almost certainly will spend more of their childhood watching movies than reading, be educated in our schools about how film works, what filmmakers do to manipulate people, and what a cut means, technically, emotionally and poetically. The engine of film cannot yet drive us to promised lands, but it could involve us in catastrophic accidents, and we have to know how that engine works.

> "On evenings with high attendance of violent movies, potential criminals are in the movie theater, and hence incapacitated from committing crimes."

Movie Violence May Decrease Violent Crime

Gordon Dahl and Stefano DellaVigna

In the following viewpoint, Gordon Dahl and Stefano DellaVigna maintain that violent movies may actually decrease crime by attracting potential criminals and incapacitating them in theaters. Dahl and DellaVigna insist that box-office attendances of strongly violent, mildly violent, and nonviolent movies correlate with crime rates, declaring that assaults decline during highly attended showings of strongly violent movies during evening weekend hours. This counters several scientific studies claiming that violent media arouse aggressive behavior, the authors conclude. Dahl is an associate professor of economics at the University of San Diego, California. DellaVigna is an assistant professor of economics at the University of Berkeley, California.

Gordon Dahl and Stefano DellaVigna, "Introduction," *Does Movie Violence Increase Violent Crime?* December 20, 2007. Reproduced by permission of the authors.

As you read, consider the following questions:

1. According to Dahl and DellaVigna, what evidence has existing research on media violence and aggression produced?
2. How do the authors define "catharsis"?
3. As stated by the authors, how many assaults are prevented each year by violent movies?

D oes violence in the media trigger violent crime? This question is important for policy and scientific research alike. In 2000, the Federal Trade Commission issued a report at the request of the President and of Congress, surveying the scientific evidence and warning of risks. In the same year, the American Medical Association, together with five other public-health organizations, issued a joint statement on the risks of exposure to media violence.

Warnings about media violence are largely based on psychological research. As [researchers Craig A.] Anderson and [Brad J.] Bushman summarize it, "Five decades of research into the effects of exposure to violent television and movies have produced thoroughly documented [. . .] research findings. It is now known that even brief exposure to violent TV or movie scenes causes significant increases in aggression, [. . .] and that media violence is a significant risk factor in youth violence. [. . .] The consistency of findings within and between the three types of TV- and movie-violence studies makes this one of the strongest research platforms in all of psychology." Other surveys reach similar conclusions.

The Unanswered Question of Crime

This research, however, stops short of establishing a causal impact of media violence on crime. The evidence from psychology . . . of two types. A first set of experiments . . . expose subjects (typically kids) to short, violent video clips. These experiments find a sharp increase in aggressive behavior immediately after the media exposure, compared to a control group. This literature provides causal evidence on the short-run impact of media violence on aggressiveness, but not on crime.

A second literature shows that survey respondents who watched more violent media are substantially more likely to be involved in self-reported violence and crime. This second type of evidence, while indeed linking media violence and crime, is plagued by problems of endogeneity and reverse causation. In sum, the research in psychology does not answer the question about media violence and crime.

In this [viewpoint], we attempt to provide causal evidence on the short-run effect of media violence on violent crime. We exploit the natural experiment induced by time-series variation in the violence of movies shown in the theater. As in the psychology experiments, we estimate the impact of exposure to violence in the short-run. Unlike in the experiments, our outcome variable is violent crime, rather than aggressiveness in the laboratory.

We measure the violence content of movies using a 0–10 rating developed by *kids-in-mind.com*, a non-profit organization. Combining the rating of movies with their daily revenue, we generate a daily measure of box office audience for strongly violent (e.g., *Hannibal*), mildly violent (e.g., *Spider-Man*), and non-violent movies (e.g., *Runaway Bride*). Since blockbuster movies differ significantly in violence rating, and movie sales are concentrated in the initial weekends since release of a movie, there is substantial variation in exposure to movie violence over time. The box office audience for strongly violent movies is as high as 10 million people on some weekends, and is close to zero on others. Since movie attendance is concentrated on weekends we focus the analysis on Fridays, Saturdays, and Sundays.

Using this variation, we estimate the same-day impact of exposure to violent movies on violent crime, holding constant the total movie audience. We use crime data from the National Incident Based Reporting System (NIBRS) for the years 1995–2004. We measure violent crime on a given day using all reported assaults (simple or aggravated) and intimidation. Since our measure of movie violence does not vary across cities, we use the total number of assaults on a given day as our outcome measure.

Violent Behavior in the Short-Run

Our initial findings offer little support for the theory that exposure to violence increases violent behavior in the short-run. After controlling flexibly for seasonality, we find that, on days with a high audience for violent movies, violent crime is lower, though not significantly so. This negative correlation may be due to unobserved variables that contemporaneously increase movie attendance and decrease violence, such as rainy weather. To address this possibility, we use two strategies. First, we add a flexible set of weather controls. Second, and most importantly, we instrument for movie audience on day t using the predicted movie audience based on the following weekend's audience. This instrumental variable strategy exploits the predictability of the weekly decrease in attendance. Adding the weather controls and instrumenting does not solve the apparent puzzle: the correlation between movie violence and violent crime becomes more negative and statistically significant.

To interpret this puzzling result, we separately estimate the effect on crime in four 6-hour blocks. As expected, we find that exposure to violent movies has no impact on crime in the morning hours (6AM–12PM) or in the afternoon (12PM–6PM); indeed, movie attendance in these hours is minimal. In the evening hours (6PM–12AM), instead, we detect a significant negative effect on crime. For each million people watching a strongly violent movie, violent crimes decrease by 0.86 percent. We find a smaller, but still sizeable and significant, impact of exposure to mildly violent movies. There is no impact of exposure to non-violent movies. We interpret these re-

A Person's Character Influences Behavior

Dr. Simon Moore teaches psychology at London Metropolitan University and is an expert on movie violence. He says: "Some experts say watching violent movies has no effect on a person, while some say it does. But very few say that people will watch a very violent film and then go out and chop someone up. The problem is that critics tend to focus on the films rather than the person who is watching them. It is a person's character that will regulate how they react. If film violence really begat violence, then people would be assaulting each other in the aisles.

"Look at the statistics—the number of people who have been inspired to carry out violence is miniscule. The media, however, exaggerate it."

Ross Chainey, "Do Violent Movies Make Violent People?"
Accessed September 17, 2008. http://style.uk.msn.com.

sults as incapacitation. On evenings with high attendance of violent movies, potential criminals are in the movie theater, and hence incapacitated from committing crimes. The magnitudes of the effects are consistent with incapacitation, provided that potential criminals sort into more violent movies.

Violent Movies Continue to Decrease Violent Behavior

We then present evidence for the morning hours following the movie showing (12AM–6AM), when most movie theaters are closed. This allows us to measure the short-run effect of movie exposure beyond the mechanical incapacitation. This measure is the field equivalent of the laboratory measurement of aggression following exposure to violent media. Over this time period, the effect of exposure to movie violence is even more negative. For each million people watching a strongly violent movie, violent crimes decrease by 1.47 percent. The effect is slightly smaller for exposure to mildly violent movies. Nonviolent movies have no significant impact. Unlike in the psychology experiments, therefore, media violence appears to decrease violent behavior in the immediate aftermath of exposure.

Before we test for interpretations of this second finding, we examine its robustness. We present disaggregate effects by two-hour time blocks, and by individual violence levels ranging from 0 to 10. We also allow for non-linear specifications. . . . The results are all consistent with the baseline analysis. We find similar results (although less precisely estimated) using an alternative measure of movie violence based on the reasons provided for the MPAA's [Motion Picture Association of America's] ratings. We also show the impact of movie violence depends on the current movie audience, rather than last week's, or next week's audience. Additionally, we generate a placebo data set to test for uncontrolled seasonal factors in movie releases. We find no evidence of a negative effect for violent movies on violent crime in this placebo treatment. A final set of results exploits the variation in movie violence from rentals of DVDs and VHSs over the years 1995–2004. These estimates are mostly consistent with our main estimates using the box office data, although the standard errors are large.

Three Main Interpretations

We discuss three main interpretations for the negative impact of violent movies on crime in the early morning hours. (i) *Extended Incapacitation.* Exposure to movies lowers crime temporarily even after the end of the movie: by the time a potential criminal exits the movie theater, the situational opportunities to engage in violent crime are diminished. (ii) *Sobriety*. Theater attendance reduces the consumption of alcohol, which in turn reduces the incidence of violent crime both during and after the movie. (iii) *Catharsis*. The viewing of movie violence has a cathartic effect, freeing tensions away from violent acts. This is an explanation in line with Aristotle's explanation in his *Poetics* of the nature of the Greek tragedy.

A key difference between the first two explanations and the Catharsis explanation is whether the effect is due exclusively to exposure to violent movies. To test for the Catharsis explanation, we look at non-violent movies which attract a demographic group more likely to commit crime: young males. We create this measure using the fraction of IMDB [Internet Movie Database] online movie ratings coming from 18 to 29 males. We find that, even after controlling for movie violence, exposure to movies that attract this group significantly lowers violent crime both in the evening hours (6PM–12AM) and in the morning (12AM–6AM). The point estimates of the impact are similar to the point estimates for the movie violence measures.

This suggests that the impact of violent movies on crime is more likely to be due to Displacement or Sobriety, rather than Catharsis (unless non-violent movies also have cathartic effects). To test the Sobriety hypothesis, we examine crime where alcohol was reported as a contributing factor. Consistent with this hypothesis, we find a larger displacement effect for assaults in which the criminal was under the influence of alcohol. We also find very large displacement for assaults taking place in bars and night clubs, although these estimates are very imprecise given the relative rarity of such assaults.

We then evaluate the magnitudes of the findings and provide interpretations. A simple calibration of the results indicates that violent movies decrease assaults by roughly 175 occurrences per day, for an annual total of about 64,000 assaults prevented. While these calibrated estimates depend on several assumptions and have a margin of error, they nonetheless suggest a very different conclusion compared to the experimental literature in psychology, which finds large positive effects.

The Long-Term Impact

A key limitation of our research design is that we cannot answer the question of the long-run impact of media violence. To the extent that exposure to violence slowly generates habituation or imitation in the long-run, we are unable to detect these effects in our short-run window. Our study, however, can address a major interpretation of the psychology evidence. *Several experiments* suggest that the impact of media violence on aggression is due to arousal. If this were the case, the impact on violent crime should peak in the hours following exposure to movie violence, contrary to what we find in the data.

These explanations also suggest two reasons why the results in the field and in the laboratory are different. First, the design of the exposure to violence is very different in laboratory studies and in the field. In the laboratory, exposure to violent (versus non-violent) media neither logistically displaces possibilities for aggression, nor reduces alcohol consumption. Further, the violent clips used in the experiments typically consist of 5–10 minutes of sequences of extreme violence. In the field, instead, actual media violence also includes meaningful acts of reconciliation, apprehension of criminals, and non-violent sequences. Second, the laboratory experiments do not take into account sorting into violent media. The experimental subjects are exposed to extreme violence that they had neither demanded nor anticipated. Individuals watching violent movies at the movie theater, instead, pay for such exposure, possibly because they are looking for a way to channel tensions. Moreover, if this self-selected group is already desensitized to violence, the marginal impact of an additional violent movie may be smaller.

> *"The most popular movies of the last two decades often show normative depictions of negative health behaviours."*

The Film Industry May Influence At-Risk Behavior

Hasantha Gunasekera, Simon Chapman, and Sharon Campbell

According to Hasantha Gunasekera, Simon Chapman, and Sharon Campbell in the following viewpoint, popular movies frequently depict unprotected sex and drug and alcohol use as consequence-free or even in a positive light. This may shape unhealthy attitudes toward at-risk behaviors and create unrealistic social norms. Therefore, the authors encourage the film industry to depict the possible repercussions of casual sex and drug and alcohol use. Gunasekera is a research fellow at the Institute of Child Health Research. Chapman is a professor in the School of Public Health at the University of Sydney, Australia. Campbell is an assistant professor in biochemistry at East Tennessee State University.

Hasantha Gunasekera, Simon Chapman, and Sharon Campbell, "Sex and Drugs in Popular Movies: An Analysis of the Top 200 Films," *Journal of the Royal Society of Medicine*, vol. 98, October 2005, pp. 464–470. Reproduced by permission.

As you read, consider the following questions:

1. Why are restrictions of tobacco advertising and smoking in movies important to Gunasekera, Chapman, and Campbell's viewpoint?

2. What examples do the authors provide for the glorification of promiscuous behavior in movies?

3. According to the authors, what fraction of the 200 movies they analyzed did not depict sex and drug and alcohol use?

The movie industry influences the perceptions of billions of people around the world. The top 200 movies in cinematic history have grossed in excess of $70 billion US dollars in box office takings alone: with globalization and the proliferation of home-based media technologies movies are becoming ever more accessible to wider audiences. Movies often address and depict health-related behaviours and have the potential to model conduct and communicate normative propositions about matters such as unsafe sex and recreational drug use as well as health-promoting messages about these issues.

The World Health Organization (WHO) reported that in 2003 there were over 40 million people living with HIV/AIDS including 5 million newly infected with HIV. Addressing this problem in part requires population behaviour change relating to unsafe sexual practices and injected drug use. Social Cognitive Theory suggests that social norms are an important factor to consider when advocating behaviour change. Observation of influential role models and the consequences of their actions affects our behaviour. This observational learning contributes to the individual's confidence in their own ability to change their behaviour. However, public health campaigns advocating safe sex practices are often not complemented by social campaigns designed to change the social norm of unprotected sex.

Despite the magnitude of the HIV/AIDS problem only around half of American men who have sex with men and who use injected drugs report that they always use a condom. Indeed, given recall bias, this figure is likely to be inflated. Condoms are the most effective method to reduce the spread of sexually transmitted diseases (STDs) other than celibacy, and their use is advocated by international bodies including the Centers for Disease Control and WHO. Despite this knowledge, condoms are consistently not the norm in sexual practice.

Convincing Evidence

There is convincing evidence that the entertainment media influences behaviour. This explains why product placement is an important form of advertising for tobacco companies. Smoking in movies promotes the uptake of smoking by adolescents and a dose-response relationship has been demonstrated for television viewing and initiation of smoking in the young. This has led to the call to use ratings to restrict access to movies with smoking. An association has been posited between television viewing and alcohol consumption in adolescents. A survey of American teenagers who engaged in risky behaviours, including sexual intercourse and drug use, showed they spent more time watching television than their peers. Recently, there has been renewed concern about the impact on children of constant exposure to violence in the mass media, reflecting concerns raised by the Surgeon General of America three decades ago.

There is a paucity of data specifically addressing popular movies and their impact on population sexual and drug taking behaviour. The recent National Youth Anti-Drug Media Campaign content analysis found that most popular movies depicted alcohol and smoking and many depicted illicit drug use. Cross-sectional survey data have shown an association between black adolescent American females' exposure to X-rated

movies and negative attitudes towards safe sex practices. Given that adolescents spend between 3–6 hours every day watching various forms of media entertainment (more time than any activity except sleep), a better understanding of the content of these messages is long overdue.

We used the Internet Movie Database [www.imdb.com] list of the top 200 movies of all time worldwide, from 30 September 2003. This list was produced using international box office gross receipts without adjusting for inflation. Our assumption was that box office takings were a proxy for viewing numbers. [The list was then reduced to 87 to include only live-action, HIV era movies with ratings more mature than PG.] . . .

Results of the Analysis

Sixty-five of 87 movies (75%) depicted a negative health behaviour defined as: unprotected sex (32%); use of cannabis [marijuana] (8%); non-injected illicit drug use (7%); smoking (68%); or alcohol intoxication (32%). Assuming all excluded movies had no incidents showing sex or drug use, at least a third (33%) of the 200 most popular movies of the last 20 years depicted negative health behaviours.

There were 28 movies that depicted one to seven episodes of sexual intercourse, giving a total of 53 individual episodes. Depictions were, typically, new heterosexual adult partners engaging in vaginal sex (40% episodes). There was one scene of homosexual (oral) sex.

There were 16 movies which depicted unprotected sex between new partners and a further 11 which depicted unprotected sex between married, *de facto* or regular partners. There was only a single sex episode in which condoms were assumed to have been used, given a previous discussion between the characters, but no episodes of definitive use. This single episode was also the only time any form of birth control was used in the 45 episodes of sex which could have resulted in pregnancy. Therefore, in 98% of sexual episodes in which pregnancy was a possible outcome, no form of birth control was used or suggested.

In 47 of 53 sex episodes (89%) no clear consequences were portrayed. In two episodes there were social problems for the characters, such as marital discord from discovered infidelity, and social embarrassment. In two episodes a partner was murdered during the act (one was a rape). In one episode a participant was injured by violent but consensual sex. In one episode a car accident resulted from oral sex while driving. None of the movies portrayed HIV transmission, other STDs or unwanted pregnancies.

There were several references to condoms using terms such as 'rubbers' and 'protection'. There were also some references to the spread of STDs ('disease-spreading whore' and 'I get checked every month'). Promiscuous behaviour was glorified ('I got laid 23 times this year', 'He's called rabbit 'cos he likes to f--- a lot') and celibacy was ridiculed ('If he decides to take the lock off his c---'). There were scant references to birth control (robot prostitute: 'You're not going to get us pregnant').

Seven of the 87 movies (8%) depicted between one and 10 episodes of cannabis usage (mean=3.9, SD=3.58). There were a total of 27 distinct episodes which involved mainly adult characters (74%) who were not in main roles (77%). Cannabis usage was shown in a positive light in 14 episodes (52%), a neutral light in 13 (48%), with no negative depictions. There were no negative consequences from cannabis use depicted.

Six of the 87 movies (7%) depicted non-injected illicit drug use. Within those movies the number of episodes of non-injected illicit drug use ranged between one and five episodes (mean=2.2, SD=1.60), with a total of 13 individual episodes. Depictions were typically of an older adult in a background role and portrayed in a positive light. In three of the 13 episodes the portrayal was neutral but none of the portrayals were considered to be negative. The only consequence depicted was a murdered addict.

At least one character was seen smoking in 59 (68%) of the movies and intoxicated with alcohol in 28 (32%). No movies depicted injected drug use. . . .

Normative Depictions of Negative Health Behaviours

This study highlights how popular movies over the last two decades have commonly depicted negative health behaviours such as unprotected sex between new partners, cannabis use, non-injected drug use, smoking, and alcohol intoxication. Only one in four movies reviewed was free from any of these depictions. It is remarkable that although one in three popular movies depicted sexual intercourse there was only one instance in which a condom may have been used. This is despite sexual intercourse rarely being depicted in monogamous relationships.

There were no references to important consequences of unsafe sex such as HIV transmission, spread of other STDs or unwanted pregnancy. The only consequences depicted were arguably irrelevant to public health (e.g. social embarrassment). Comments made by characters during the movies reinforced promiscuity and ridiculed monogamy and celibacy consistent with previous research.

Movies depicted drug use far less commonly than unprotected sex, with the exception of smoking (68%) and alcohol intoxication (32%). These findings reinforce previous studies that have documented the prevalence of smoking and alcohol in the mass media. However, a previous study reported a higher proportion of movies (98%) depicting negative health behaviours. This was due to their inclusion of any alcohol consumption and any use of over-the-counter or prescription medicines. This is the first study to demonstrate both the tendency to depict the use of these drugs in a positive light and not to depict any consequences arising from the use of these drugs. Interestingly cannabis tended to be used by younger characters and injected drug use was absent, perhaps reflecting the target audiences.

A recent analysis of sex on television found that fewer (14%) shows depicted or strongly implied sexual intercourse than we found in movies. However, an increasing number (15%) included a safe sex message contrasting with our findings.

Deciding whether a scene depicts a sexual encounter and whether safe sex practices were adopted will always be subjective. Different audiences can sometimes interpret the same scenes differently and discerning this was beyond the scope of our study. Data are required on how different subpopulations respond to the public health messages in the media and which sub-populations are watching what movies. Such analyses would be more appropriately conducted using different methodologies (e.g. focus groups). We also acknowledge that no attempt was made to differentiate fleeting depictions with more influential prolonged depictions of the negative health behaviours we studied.

The regular exposure to unprotected sex with new partners and recreational drug use by influential movie stars in combination with an absence of negative consequence from these actions must be considered in the context of the difficulty experienced by public health advocates in changing population behaviours. This observational learning, using Social Cognitive Theory, may exert a significant competing influence to the safe sex and 'just say no' messages propounded by some optimistic public health officials. Unsafe sex and recreational drug use in movies could potentially have a similar effect to the influence of media on smoking, alcohol and violent behaviours.

The most popular movies of the last two decades often show normative depictions of negative health behaviours. The motion picture industry should be encouraged to depict safer sex practices and to depict the real consequences of unprotected sex and illicit drug use.

> *"Feeding us biased studies about the supposed evils of silly movies is unhelpful at best, and at worst diverts energy and support away from legitimate public-health concerns."*

The Film Industry Should Not Be Blamed for At-Risk Behavior

David Goldenberg

In the following viewpoint, David Goldenberg argues that a major study linking popular movies to risky sexual behavior and substance abuse uses shoddy statistics and distorted data to hold Hollywood responsible for public health issues. Goldenberg alleges that the number of films portraying marijuana use is inflated and depictions of condom usage and the consequences of AIDS are blatantly overlooked in the study. Therefore, he insists that even if moviegoers looked to Hollywood for public health cues instead of entertainment, the study's flaws undermine its own claims. Goldenberg is cofounder and editor of Gelf, *an online news magazine.*

As you read, consider the following questions:

1. In Goldenberg's view, why is the study's analysis of only the top-grossing movies flawed?

2. As described by the author, why is the study's coding of sexual intercourse manipulative?

3. What safe-sex and STD-transmission portrayals did the study overlook, according to Goldenberg?

A new study in the October [2005] issue of the *Journal of the Royal Society of Medicine* reviews the top-grossing movies worldwide and concludes: "The most popular movies of the last two decades often show normative depictions of negative health behaviours. The motion picture industry should be encouraged to depict safer sex practices and to depict the real consequences of unprotected sex and illicit drug use."

Serious Flaws in the Data Collection

Yes, a respected medical journal published a paper that involves doctors and research assistants taking detailed notes on lots of movies in an effort to determine whether Jason Biggs et al. wore condoms. And, yes, the study does try to blame Hollywood for normalizing "negative health behaviours." But even if we disregard the fact that people don't necessarily take their public-health cues from films like *Scary Movie* and *Rambo: First Blood Part II*, the study has serious flaws that undermine even its tenuous claim on our attention.

Though the title of the paper is "Sex and drugs in popular, movies: an analysis of the top 200 films," the paper only deals with 87 films—those that were produced and set in the last 20 years and have a rating above PG. While the reviewers explain why they did this—they discarded animated movies, films that took place in the pre-HIV era, and those that were unlikely to depict sexual acts—they often fail to explain how this artificially increases their numbers. (The 39 movies excluded because they were filmed or set before the HIV era may well have depicted sex and drug use, but the 74 G- and PG-rated flicks and animated films probably didn't. Shouldn't Hollywood get credit for those?)

For example, a BBC [British Broadcasting Corporation] article about the study notes: "Movies with cannabis [marijuana] (8%) and other non-injected illicit drugs (7%) were less common than those with alcohol intoxication (32%) and tobacco use (68%), but tended to portray their use positively and without negative consequences, the researchers said." Those percentages are of the movies that the researchers pre-selected as movies that would be likely to have these events in them, so the stats are virtually meaningless. If the excluded 113 movies didn't show marijuana usage, then only seven of the top 200, or 3.5%, show any form of toking. (The public-health concerns raised by marijuana usage are scant, at best, but that's a topic for another day.)

The quote from the BBC article comes directly from the press release issued by the *Journal of the Royal Society of Medicine*, as does most of the rest of the article. Certainly, press-release plagiarism is more the BBC's fault than the journal's, but the fact that the journal so willfully distorts data is cause for concern.

Hollywood Is Not to Blame

Moreover, researchers chose these films from the top 200 grossing films of all time, according to the "All-Time Worldwide Box Office" list at IMDB.com [Internet Movie Database]. As Dr. Hasantha Gunasekera, the University of Sydney clinical research fellow who is first author on the paper, notes (in both the press release and the BBC article), these movies are important because they "have grossed in excess of $70 billion US dollars [£39 billion] in box office takings." But it's not up to Hollywood to decide who goes to see what films. *Gelf* [magazine] is not sure how different the list would be if, say, the researchers instead focused on the films that had cost the most to make, but the point is that the researchers looked at outcome, not intent, and then blamed the movie makers. Maybe people would simply rather see escapist movies that didn't stop to explain that a pus-filled infection could result from careless sex. There are plenty of serious movies with major actors who suffer consequences as a result of unprotected sex, and it's not Hollywood's fault that more people want to see *There's Something About Mary* than *Philadelphia*.

And the researchers certainly biased their results by using the director's cuts and extended versions of the movies they were studying, which they stated "were viewed in preference to standard releases." Anyone who's bought one of those DVDs recently knows that they are generally unrated boobfests, and can be very different from what was shown in theaters.

Gunasekera et al. were also looking only at international box-office receipts; it's not exactly Hollywood's fault that international distributors tend to pick up the crappiest flicks for worldwide distribution. If they had focused on IMDB's "All-Time USA" box office list, for example, they would have found a few movies with more drug and sex-related consequences (like *Traffic*) to go along with the requisite Adam Sandler movies. (Surprisingly, the study's authors decided not to adjust for inflation, either, when selecting their box-office hits; instead they just used IMDB's list. By not adjusting for inflation, researchers might miss movies seen by more people back when movie tickets were cheaper. *Gelf* isn't sure how the adjustment would have changed the results, but it does indicate a bit of laziness.)

Untrustworthy Methods

Throughout the study, the researchers consistently manipulated their data in ways that would make movies appear to be sinister agents of poor public health. Here's how they coded sexual acts:

Not All Youths Are Affected

Research suggests that not all youths are affected in the same way by viewing media violence. Factors that appear to influence the effects of media violence on aggressive or violent behavior include characteristics of the viewer (such as age, intelligence, aggressiveness, and whether the child perceives the media as realistic and identifies with aggressive characters) and his or her social environment (for example, parental influences), as well as aspects of media content (including characteristics of perpetrators, degree of realism and justification for violence, and depiction of consequences of violence).

Evidence that these factors moderate the influence of media violence is limited, and it is more relevant to aggression than to violence. For example, studies of responses to violent television and films and violent video games have found that people who were initially more aggressive than other subjects were more affected in behavior, thoughts, and emotions. Research in this area clearly suggests that the impact of violent television, film, and video games on aggression is moderated by viewers' aggressive characteristics. Evidence that other individual, environmental, and content factors moderate the effects of exposure to media violence is less clear. Some studies suggest that these factors may buffer or enhance effects, but few have tested for such influences.

David Satcher,
"Youth Violence: A Report of the Surgeon General,"
January 17, 2001. http://mentalhealth.samhsa.gov.

Defining an act of sexual intercourse presented coding challenges as these movies were designed for mass release to worldwide audiences and rarely depicted explicit scenes. Reviewers were instructed to code any episode in which an overtly sexual physical encounter either took place or was implied which could potentially result in an unwanted pregnancy or the transmission of an STD [sexually transmitted disease].

They included any implied scene of sex, yet they also demanded that birth control use be explicit, not just implied. In other words, even if a couple is humping offscreen, the researchers counted it as "no condom" unless the condom was onscreen. They were very serious about this; *Gelf* finds it hilarious to picture these researchers intently focusing on the screen and on the sex acts. "Two reviewers watched each film to minimize omissions due to concentration lapses," according to the paper.

They claim that of the 53 sex scenes—implied or otherwise—in the movies they watched, there was only a single coupling in which condoms were assumed to have been used. They also claim, "This single episode was also the only time any form of birth control was used in the 45 episodes of sex which could have resulted in pregnancy." They later add, "None of the movies portrayed HIV transmission, other STDs or unwanted pregnancies."

The condom "episode" occurs in *Pretty Woman*, when Julia Roberts offers Richard Gere his choice of condom colors. I guess the zoom-in on the condom wrapper during the *coitus interruptus* [the withdrawal method of contraception] scene at the start of *American Pie 2* didn't make it into their charts. Nor did Jenny's death from AIDS in *Forrest Gump*.

The Study Admits to Subjectivity

In order to make sure their data was accurate and to test interobserver reliability, the authors had both research teams code a group of the 10 movies. They found several conflicting results, including 15 instances where one team had coded a sex act as involving "no condom" and the other team had coded "don't know." That didn't seem to tone down their conclusions: "Importantly," they wrote, "there were no disagreements between the teams as to whether condoms were used. . . ."

Even more confusing? In the conclusions, they wrote, "Deciding whether a scene depicts a sexual encounter and whether safe sex practices were adopted will always be subjective. Different audiences can sometimes interpret the same scenes differently and discerning this was beyond the scope of our study." *Gelf* thought this was exactly the scope of their study. There are certainly important things to say about how popular culture and public health intertwine. But feeding us biased studies about the supposed evils of silly movies is unhelpful at best, and at worst diverts energy and support away from legitimate public-health concerns.

> *"Given the absence of Americans of color in key positions, it is not surprising that the views offered by Hollywood are often misinformed or thoroughly white-washed."*

Hollywood Films Are Racist

Joe R. Feagin

Joe R. Feagin is a sociologist and the Ella C. McFadden Professor of Liberal Arts at Texas A&M University. In the following viewpoint, he argues that the Hollywood film industry has not fully shed its racist past. Although the civil rights movement dramatically improved cinematic portrayals of African Americans and other minorities, Feagin contends that white men continue to control the mass media and that most major motion pictures depict white identity and institutions as positive and heroic in settings of slavery and widespread racism. Furthermore, the author insists that many white Americans and audiences worldwide still buy into these racial images created by Hollywood studios.

As you read, consider the following questions:

1. How does Feagin support his assertion that for the average American movies are a greater source of knowledge than books and magazines?

Joe R. Feagin, *Screen Saviors: Hollywood Fictions of Whiteness*. Lanham, MD: Rowman & Littlefield Publishers, Inc., 2003. Copyright © 2003 by Rowman & Littlefield Publishers, Inc. All rights reserved. Reproduced by permission.

2. According to the author, why is *Amistad* a racist movie?

3. In the author's view, how have Hollywood movies shaped recent immigrants' attitudes toward black Americans?

Hollywood movies are much more than a matter of entertainment. Hollywood has become a major educational institution. For the majority of Americans, Hollywood's movies are a constant source of images, ideas, and data about the social world. Indeed, the average citizen spends about 13 hours a year at movie theaters, and half of all adults go to the movies at least once a month. Even more significant, given the country's multiracial future, is the fact that a majority of younger Americans view going to movies as very important in their lives, and more than six in ten watch at least one movie video a week. Almost all U.S. families now have a VCR, and watching movies is the top leisure-time activity. Americans spend a large portion of their waking time watching movies in theaters and on television, far more time than they spend on other sources of information such as magazines and books.

The Media Elite

Some social commentators view this media-drenched situation as a great achievement in human communication, as a major enlightenment of humanity and a support for democracy. Yet, moviemaking and the other mass media are today controlled by a very small and quite undemocratic elite, one that is substantially concerned with maintaining current class, racial, and gender arrangements. This media elite is a major generator and reinforcer of the ideologies that rationalize the social hierarchies of this very unequal society. This elite has long dominated the creation and dissemination of system-rationalizing ideas by means of the mass media, politics, the schools, and the churches. Today, the mass media, including movie theaters and television, provide powerful tools to disseminate this system-rationalizing ideology in its many subtle and blatant forms.

Who are the members of the U.S. moviemaking elite? Today, just a few dozen people, almost all of them white men, run the movie business. All are at the helm of companies that are part of very large media conglomerates. Women and people of color have, at best, a marginal presence in the shaping of moviemaking and most other media enterprises. Many of the white male moviemakers are relatively liberal in their personal politics; yet when it comes to racial matters . . . they still offer up a mostly sanitized and whitewashed view of the racial and other social history of the United States. There are, of course, few actors, writers, and directors of color in their midst to counter white prejudices and stereotypes about social worlds. Indeed, over the years many white, male movie executives have participated in limiting the role of, or discriminating against, African American actors, directors, and writers. Other than a few token black stars such as Halle Berry or Denzel Washington, most of Hollywood's productions today employ few African Americans or other Americans of color in influential positions. Given the absence of Americans of color in key positions, it is not surprising that the views offered by Hollywood are often misinformed or thoroughly whitewashed. . . .

Early Movies Established the Racial Divide

In some early films, such as the much-heralded *Birth of a Nation* (1915) celebrating the Ku Klux Klan, images of African Americans are viciously racial caricatures. Early white moviemakers made no attempt to portray African Americans or their lives realistically. In these movies, white Americans are always the heroes and African Americans are portrayed as villains, cheerleaders, or bystanders to white history-making.

In regard to racial imaging, perhaps the most influential Hollywood film ever made is *Gone with the Wind* (1939), an extraordinarily popular and still money-making film. It is today shown many times a day and in countless countries around the world. This movie has played a central role in communicating to Americans of many different backgrounds, as well as to people in other countries, what U.S. history (the Civil War) and U.S. racial relations are supposed to be about, from a white perspective. . . . All the heroes in this racist film are white, whereas the black characters are mostly stereotyped as loyal servants or mammies. . . . This movie has, for many decades, helped to shape basic images of white and black Americans. Although these early racist movies purport to tell U.S. history, they are basically social propaganda films for the white supremacist view of U.S. history. Their racist fantasies have often been taken for the real world. As the movie critic James Snead put it, filmmaking can, "governed by the film maker's will, imagination, and ideological slant, present a fantasy or ideal world that has nothing to do with the real world, but present it *as if it were the real world.*"

White Supremacy Is Maintained

Moving on to more recent movies . . . there has been a significant decline in crudely racist images of African Americans in Hollywood movies since the late 1950s. Yet this shift in images of African Americans has for the most part *not* been accompanied by a changed image of white society and white institutions. In more recent movies such as *Guess Who's Coming to Dinner* (1967) and *Glory* (1990), the images of African Americans have changed very significantly from those of *Birth of a Nation* and *Gone with the Wind*. Recent, more liberal movie portraits do now encompass the intelligence, bravery, seriousness, and commitment of African Americans. Of course, this major change has not come mainly as the result of generosity on the part of the moviemaking elite but rather from the

A Demeaning White Stereotype

[2007's *Dreamgirls*] props up the tired old stereotype of the uptight white nerd, hopelessly incapable of the grit and authenticity effortlessly generated by other hues. Due to constant repetition in commercials, movies and comedy acts, this demeaning white stereotype has become largely normalized in our society. How would we feel if the racial positions were switched, and a film about sympathetic white musicians cut from their enjoyable performance to a raucous scene on the chitlin circuit? What if it mockingly presented hyper-sexualized black bodies undulating wildly and sporting shabby clothing?

Jesse Adams,
"Hollywood-Sanctioned Racism Perpetuates Prejudice,"
February 7, 2007. www.browndailyherald.com.

pressures of African American and other civil rights demonstrators who have protested racial discrimination in the United States since the 1950s.

In contrast to the changing images of African Americans over the course of nearly a century of movies, Hollywood images of whites—and especially white institutions—have stayed much the same. In the late 1900s and early 2000s, as in the early 1900s, the movie image of the ideal white self is always pushed to the center, and it is consistently a white self that is good, brave, generous, and powerful. In *Guess Who's Coming to Dinner*, for example, it is the white patriarch (Spencer Tracy) who dominates the tension in the picture and who, in the end, chooses the racially tolerant option he earlier rejected, thereby upholding the "sincere fiction" of the good white man yet one more time in the movies.

A Heroic White Self

In addition, a number of major Hollywood movies have shown a heroic white self that is a type of "messiah" figure for people of color, a white figure that saves the latter from misfortune. This is true of *Glory*, which centers disproportionately on the white commander of a black military unit. When racial matters appear in Hollywood films, the images of white superiority and virtue almost always remain central.

Even in the path-breaking Hollywood movie about a revolt by enslaved Africans, *Amistad* (1997) . . . the central hero is still a white male messiah, in this case U.S. president John Quincy Adams. Although the movie presents the horrors of the slave ships for the first time in a mainstream movie, and has an admirable black hero in Cinqué, the leader of the enslaved Africans, it deals with the brutality of slavery by focusing on a rare event when U.S. legal institutions supported the freeing of enslaved Africans. The only reason this Supreme Court decision went the way it did was because the Africans concerned were *not* owned by U.S. slaveholders but by foreign slaveholders. In fact, virtually all *those same white-controlled institutions* worked hard to keep African *Americans* fully enslaved in this period. It is Adams whose speech to the Supreme Court is seen as the messiah-like moment in the film that results in the Court's freeing the Africans. Although slavery is no longer romanticized, U.S. legal institutions are indeed romanticized, and major aspects of U.S. racism are once again swept under the rug. . . .

From the *Birth of a Nation* to the latest Hollywood films, whites as a group have almost always been portrayed as morally and intellectually superior and as meritorious. In recent movies, a few white bigots may appear, yet contemporary society is not shown to be institutionally racist. In few movies is there a serious acknowledgment of the seamy racist side of contemporary society.

Significantly, there is much unity of approach in Hollywood on these racial matters. . . . Yet virtually all the movies they have made fit the same mold of not challenging white privilege and the racist character of U.S. institutions. Some recent Hollywood movies do question the actions of some racist white individuals, but only a *very* few (*Little Big Man, Bulworth, Lone Star*) try to raise questions about the institutional character of racism in U.S. society.

White Moviegoers Are Like Sheep

Unfortunately, recent survey data continue to show that the majority of white Americans still buy into some negative images of African Americans and into the positive view of the United States as not institutionally racist. In addition, most Americans, including most white Americans, are not well informed about important aspects of U.S. history and society. For this reason, the white-male elite can continue to misinform the general population on racial matters. Starting when they are young children, most whites come to adopt the stereotyped and prejudiced views of racial matters held by previous generations and still circulated by established authorities. Among the white authorities, since at least the 1910s and 1920s, have been the moviemakers. Today, as in the past, Hollywood movies communicate much misinformation about U.S. society. For most movie watchers, the movies still teach major lessons about class, racial, and gender understandings; reinforce and support racial and other social hierarchies; and help to perpetuate the deeply inegalitarian foundation of U.S. society.

Like sheep following their leader everywhere, most white Americans accept much of what they see in the mass media as real and use this misinformation to make judgments about the society around them. The movies have had a profound effect on the minds of many people, to the extent that many accept movie fantasies as historical reality. Even prominent

Americans have demonstrated an inability to tell the fictional accounts of the movies from real life. For example, in his 1980 campaign for the presidency, Ronald Reagan often described a "true" story about a heroic bomber pilot in World War II. According to Reagan, the pilot decided to land his badly damaged bomber because one of his men was severely injured and said the emotional words, "We'll ride it down together." Yet the account was not from historical reality but from a film, *A Wing and a Prayer*, in which Reagan had been an actor.

Very Little Has Improved

Is there hope for change in white attitudes and actions? Are more moviemakers following the lead of the few moviemakers who have occasionally challenged the racist histories, portraits, and images of this society? Sadly, there is little sign of such a change. Conformity to anti-black and other racist imaging persists today and is even becoming a global trend that is creating or reinforcing white-racist images across the world. Every minute of every day, somewhere on this planet, television stations broadcast and movie theaters show many of the most blatantly racist Hollywood movies, such *Gone with the Wind, The Little Rascals*, the many Tarzan movies, the many cowboy-and-Indian movies, and even Disney cartoon classics such as *Song of the South*. They also show the latest movies, those that continue to celebrate white Americans and white-controlled institutions. For nearly a century now, U.S. movie corporations have not only generated and reinforced racist images of Americans of color and stereotyped positive images of white Americans for those who live in the United States but also circulated these racist images in most other countries. The corporations that now control Hollywood's moviemaking and the other U.S. mass media are increasingly in charge of global education. Something like half of Europe's entertainment programs (other than sports) are based on U.S. sources. Growing billions of the world's peoples now get their entertainment from U.S. movies, television programs, and videos, as well as directly from the U.S. Armed Forces' television broadcasts and cable channels.

Boomerang Effects

The consequences of this are negative for African Americans wherever they may be. And there are boomerang effects when those who have watched U.S. movies come to the United States as immigrants. Thus, one study interviewed rural Taiwanese who had never been in the United States. While they sometimes realized that the U.S. mass media were engaged in stereotyping, most still accepted racist views of African Americans. These negative images were gleaned from U.S. movies, television shows, and music videos seen in Taiwan. Similarly, other researchers have reported that recent Latin American immigrants to the United States often have anti-black attitudes when they arrive because they have seen so many U.S. movies. Anti-black images are carried by the new immigrants into the United States and become the basis for negative attitudes toward and negative interactions with black Americans.

The U.S. movie industry is thus heavily implicated in the globalization of racism, and it has been thus implicated for several decades. . . . [A] number of reform strategies are now very much in order, if the United States and the world are to counteract this globe-circling reinforcement of racism directed at African Americans and other dark-skinned peoples. At the center of these strategies must be teaching all viewers of the movies a critical approach, one that enables them to see through and behind the creations of those moviemakers who would control our minds, imaginations, values, and practices.

> *"Evidence is there that, in unprecedented numbers, the interests and passions of minorities across the board—not just African Americans—are taking their place in the pantheon of the most popular art form in the world."*

Minority Representation in Hollywood Films Is Improving

Michael E. Ross

Michael E. Ross is a reporter for MSNBC.com and editor of its Race & Ethnicity section. Ross asserts in the following viewpoint that Hollywood has reached a "tipping point" for racial representation and equality. He claims that the recent Academy Award victories for African American actors as well as culturally diverse films are lifting minorities from their longtime marginal status on the silver screen. In Ross's view, achievement in film—and in the box office—is shifting toward merit, and this shift not only transcends race, but also gender and subject matter.

As you read, condsider the following questions:

1. What example does Ross provide for the advancement of Latinos in Hollywood?

2. What "tipping points" for African American actors occurred in 2004, in Ross's view?

3. According to the author, what trend has changed the action hero?

[Journalist] Malcolm Gladwell's 2002 best-selling book *The Tipping Point* advanced the notion that small, seemingly incidental factors can make the difference between an idea withering in the face of public indifference and exploding into a wildfire of acceptance, embraced by the public as "the next big thing."

Oscar victories for Jamie Foxx and Morgan Freeman on Sunday night [February 27, 2005], and the numerous nominations for other stars that night, may well be the long-contemplated, dreamed-about tipping point for popular culture—that moment when the still comparatively marginal status of minorities in motion pictures changed forever.

Sunday's triumphant night for African American actors and their legions of fans has been anticipated for weeks. The nominations of four black actors and five films devoted to African American characters or themes made Oscars 2005 something of a watershed for black moviegoers before the first statuettes were even handed out.

But evidence is there that, in unprecedented numbers, the interests and passions of minorities across the board—not just African Americans—are taking their place in the pantheon of the most popular art form in the world.

There's the rollicking swagger of Jamie Foxx's star turn in *Ray*; Don Cheadle's poignant, affecting portrayal in *Hotel Rwanda*; the stirring breakthrough of Catalina Sandino Moreno in *Maria Full of Grace*; and contributions from *The Motorcycle Diaries* and *House of Flying Daggers*.

There's Darrell Roodt's *Yesterday*, a study of survival and hope amidst the AIDS epidemic, and South Africa's first

Academy-nominated film (nominated for best foreign language film); *Mighty Times: The Children's March*, a study of youth activists battling segregation in 1963 (which won for short subject documentary), and Al Otra Lado del Rio (from [*The Motorcycle*] *Diaries*), the first Spanish-language song to win an Oscar.

Other Tipping Points?

There have been other signs of such progress—earlier tipping points—over the past few years:

1. In March 2002 Denzel Washington and Halle Berry won the Oscars for best actor and best actress, respectively, and Sidney Poitier received a special honorary Oscar for "remarkable accomplishments." It was a dramatic advance for black stars in Hollywood, and a new ratification of acceptance of African Americans' place in movie history.

2. That same year Arenas Entertainment, an independent film production company focused on Latino moviegoers, began a distribution and marketing partnership with Universal Pictures, the better to gain a piece of U.S. Latino purchasing power, estimated by *Hispanic Business* magazine at $500 billion a year.

3. The weekend of Aug. 6, 2004, *Collateral*, starring Tom Cruise and Jamie Foxx (in his second Oscar-nominated role) opened at No. 1 in box office receipts, followed by Denzel Washington's *The Manchurian Candidate* (No. 4), Will Smith's *I, Robot* (No. 6) and Halle Berry's *Catwoman* (No. 9). *Shrek 2*, with the vocal talents of Eddie Murphy, was at No. 18, and *King Arthur*, the medieval action film directed by African American Antoine Fuqua, was at No. 20 that weekend, a week when, for the first time, films directed by or starring African Americans in prominent roles were six of the top 20 movies Americans went to see—four of the top 10.

Asian Horror Cinema

Over the last decade or so, Asian cinema has taken over the horror film genre.... While western filmmakers continue to recycle the tame tired plots and ideas, Asian movie makers have gone into their cultural well to dig out new tropes and concepts—or, at least, new variations on very old cultural tropes.

Probably the surest indicator of ... Asian horror cinema [success] is the speed with which Hollywood is churning out remakes of Japanese and other Asian horror films—and the sizable earnings these films are raking in at the US box office.

Ashok K. Banker, "More than a Grudge *and a* Ring: Why Asian Horror Films Rock," Blogcritics, *September 22, 2005. http://blogcritics.org.*

4. Despite merciless drubbing by the critics, the new Ice Cube road comedy *Are We There Yet?* has notched more than $76.4 million in receipts, according to data from Exhibitor Relations Co. The film remains in the top 10 more than six weeks after its release.

5. And on Sunday, the comedy *Diary of a Mad Black Woman* made a surprising No. 1 box-office debut, raking in $22 million in ticket sales while still in limited release—and pushing out of the top position the Will Smith film *Hitch*, which had occupied the No. 1 spot for about three weeks before that.

For Paul Dergarabedian, whose Exhibitor Relations company monitors domestic movie box-office sales, what matters is what's on the screen—product that increasingly reflects more of America and the world.

"The hope is that the awards would become colorblind anyway, that it's about the work," he said on Oscar night from Los Angeles. "But there's a lot going on with African American actors and actresses. There's no denying that the level of talent that's out there is deserving of box-office success, and also of critical success at the awards."

"Meritocracy" of the Movies

"A movie has to be entertaining to make money," he said. "People don't go just to make a statement. Opening weekends, yes, maybe people go for different reasons. But for a film to stay in the marketplace like *Hitch* or *Are We There Yet?*, it comes down to a meritocracy. They won't be sustained in the marketplace just because they're there. That doesn't guarantee you a spot in the box office."

"For a movie to hang in there for more than one week is a function of people responding to it. Films nominated for Oscars have to have a certain power and strength to them. Otherwise it would bring the whole process down if it had nothing to do with the quality of the work.

"It's not about the popularity of these movies—this is the first time in years there hasn't been a $100 million film in the bunch—but they all deserve a chance to be in that rarefied air," he said.

Equal Opportunity Diversity

For Dergarabedian, the shift in American cinema transcends race, going on to embrace gender and topical distinctions as well.

"You can apply this to other trends, like female action figures," he said. "Twenty years ago, a female action hero couldn't get arrested. Now you have females in powerful roles kicking butt, and those films do well. A few years ago they were strictly roles for males; now the females take care of things on their own.

"There's been a tipping point on a lot of things, not only race but also subject matter," Dergarabedian said. "Consider *The Passion of the Christ* on religion, or *Fahrenheit 9/11* on politics. There are so many ways the culture is evolving and becoming accepting of different voices, different angles. There is more diversity in terms of actors, actresses and the creative side of things. And that's a good thing."

> *"Too often Hollywood has . . . succumbed to a Ramboesque parochial populism that displays naivete, ignorance and arrogance in its portrayal of the rest of the world."*

Hollywood Films Export Negative Aspects of American Culture

Nathan Gardels and Mike Medavoy

In the following viewpoint, Nathan Gardels and Mike Medavoy declare that audiences worldwide, especially in Muslim and Asian countries, are turning away from Hollywood movies because of their cultural associations with promiscuity, permissiveness, and materialism. This is largely the result of the movie industry's blockbuster formula of action and sex, Gardels and Medavoy argue. To regain their prestige and place in the global market, the authors conclude that Hollywood filmmakers must take into account the positive and negative aspects of American culture. Gardels is editor of NPQ *(New Perspectives Quarterly), an international news publication. Medavoy is chairman and chief executive officer of Phoenix Pictures, a film company.*

As you read, consider the following questions:

1. According to the authors, what is "soft power"?

2. In Gardels and Medavoy's opinion, what has eroded global sympathy for the United States?

3. How has the economic prosperity and the digital revolution affected Asian nations, in the authors' view?

The publication of cartoon depictions of the Prophet Mohammed in a Danish daily [in 2005] inflamed the pious and mobilized the militant across the Muslim world. The American casting of Chinese actresses in *Memoirs of a Geisha* stirred the considerable ire of Japanese nationalists when it was released. At a recent Rolling Stones concert in Shanghai, the Chinese government prohibited the aging rockers from singing "Let's Spend the Night Together." Indonesian Muslim activists are in an uproar over the launch of a local version of *Playboy* magazine, even though there is no nudity.

These are but the latest episodes of a clash that is a result of the globalized media crowding cultures with incommensurate values into the same public square. They suggest that, unlike past moments in history, the main conflict today is less about armies and territories than about the cultural flows of the global information economy. The core of that system is America's media-industrial complex, including Hollywood entertainment. If culture is on the front line of global affairs, then Hollywood, as much as the Pentagon or Silicon Valley, has a starring role.

Hollywood's Waning Soft Power

The reasons for Hollywood's power, which projects America's way of life to others as well as to ourselves, are clear. Long before celluloid and pixels were invented, Plato understood that "those who tell the stories also rule." Philosophers tell us that images rule dreams, and dreams rule actions. And, if music sets the mood for the multitudes, the warblings of Sinatra and Madonna are surely the Muzak of the world order.

This vast influence of American culture in the world is what Harvard professor Joseph Nye has called "soft power."

Now, however, we are witnessing a mounting resistance, particularly from Asia and the Muslim world, to the American medium's libertarian and secular messages.

There is also resistance to the mere fact of America's overwhelming cultural dominance. Josef Joffe, the publisher-editor of the German weekly *Die Zeit* has put it directly: "Between Vietnam and Iraq, America's cultural presence has expanded into ubiquity, and so has resentment of America. Soft power does not necessarily increase the world's love for America. It is still power, and it still makes enemies."

If, as Nye has said, politics in the information age is about whose story wins, America's story, which has won for so long, is losing its universal appeal. Fewer and fewer are buying into the American narrative. Needless to say, that has big implications for America's storyteller—Hollywood—as well.

America's soft power is losing its luster for several reasons. Though projected through movies and music, that power has been based fundamentally on ideals more or less realized in practice—individual freedom, the rule of law, social and economic opportunity. In foreign policy it has meant the defense of human rights, the just use of force against fascism and the containment of Soviet power.

Certainly the unilateral invasion and occupation of Iraq has fueled intense anger at America, eroding the natural sympathy after 9/11 [2001 terrorist attacks]. But perhaps more disturbing to those who once held up America as a model has been not only Guantanamo, the Abu Ghraib prison abuse and the Haditha massacre but the White House defense of torture, its dismissal of the key aspects of the Geneva protocols on treatment of prisoners of war and the government wiretapping of its own citizens.

The [Hurricane] Katrina catastrophe in New Orleans not only exposed anew unsolved racial issues but revealed to a shocked world the burgeoning inequality that has crept back into American society as the welfare state has withered.

The rise of the Christian right has made many, in Europe in particular, doubt whether a majority still shares America's founding commitment to the secular principles of the Enlightenment.

Seized by the marketing machine, Hollywood entertainment has, with ever fewer exceptions, hewn to the blockbuster formula of action, violence, sex and special effects. A masterful drama like Orson Welles' *Citizen Kane* would be impossible to make in Hollywood today. In a recent Gallup Poll of 8,000 women in Muslim countries, the overwhelming majority cited "attachment to spiritual and moral values" as the best aspect of their own societies, while the most common answer to the question about what they admired least in the West was "moral decay, promiscuity and pornography" that pollsters called "the Hollywood image."

This is also the view of many parents in the United States, no doubt including those who swell the megachurch congregations on Sunday morning and then mysteriously morph into the audience for *Desperate Housewives* on Sunday night.

Too often Hollywood has also succumbed to a Ramboesque parochial populism that displays naivete, ignorance and arrogance in its portrayal of the rest of the world.

In short, what once gilded the American experience in the eyes of much of the world now tarnishes it.

Finally, the new civilizational confidence that comes along with growing prosperity, notably in Asia, means audiences increasingly want to be entertained by their own myths and stories, not those from America. The digital distribution revolution, which is shifting power from the producer to the consumer will hasten this trend.

Hollywood Can Never Rest on Its Laurels

With the advent of new electronic distribution technologies, Hollywood is also facing a major paradigm shift that may well have important impacts on the way it and its competitors do business in the future. These technologies will eventually make it possible to dispatch films directly and cheaply to individual purchasers, thereby in principle opening up the market to more effective contestation by smaller independent production and distribution companies from a wider circle of locations. Thus, on the one hand, the advent of motion-picture distribution by means of the Internet will no doubt give rise to a great increase in the amount of cinematic material available to consumers, thereby broadening the market and almost certainly making inroads on audiences for blockbuster films. . . . Equally, there is much evidence to suggest that foreign film industries might be re-entering the competitive foray, not only on the basis of revivified local production clusters and fresh competitive strategies, but also thanks to enhanced distributional and marketing capacities aided by the rise of home-grown media conglomerates. Hollywood can never rest on its laurels.

Allen J. Scott, "Hollywood in the Era of Globalization,"
YaleGlobal, *November 29, 2002. http://yaleglobal.yale.edu.*

A Mixed Picture

To some, of course, America's image remains appealing, even a magnet for migration across scorching deserts or in the holds of rusty cargo ships; but to others it incites hatred, if not terrorism against The Great Satan. To most, though, it is a mixed picture that elicits a bit of love and loathing. As is commonly cited, Iranian or Chinese teens, for example, may embrace American pop culture but patriotically reject U.S. policies.

Movies, like politics, are a communal experience. In a democracy, the voting booth and the box office share the same public. In modern America, the media, including movies and pop music, constitute the "public square." With globalization, that is now true for the world as a whole.

To recapture its winning story in this new global politics of culture—to recover its waning soft power—America has to once again close the gap between its ideals and their practical realization that home and abroad, starting with changing our policies and getting out of Iraq. And America's storytellers need—as some indeed have—to stop seeing the world as a crowd of "extras" with turbans, burkas, slanted eyes or sombreros but no depth of character or central role.

The interplay between mass culture and public diplomacy also must be considered. In reviewing the illusions of neoconservatives that led to the debacle of preemptive war in Iraq, Francis Fukuyama, the famed author of *The End of History*, has called for a demilitarization of America's approach to the fight against jihadist terrorism and the use of more "soft power" to win over moderate Muslims. But, unfortunately, he laments, American's biggest soft-power weapon, Hollywood, only plays a negative role. "It is perceived as the purveyor of the kind of secular, materialistic, permissive culture," according to Fukuyama, "that is not very popular in many parts of the world, especially the Islamic world."

In the "long war" to win over the agitated hearts and minds of the Muslim ummah in an era in which MTV has gone where the CIA [Central Intelligence Agency] could never penetrate, any U.S. effort at public diplomacy that ignores the impact of Hollywood on the world is clueless. Karen Hughes (the [George W.] Bush confidant who is under secretary for public diplomacy) is just no match for the Britneys, Jessicas or

Angelinas of pop culture not to speak of the deeply nefarious fare that sometimes crosses the American airwaves or bristles along the fiber-optic cables.

Any effort to win over Muslims to Western ideas thus has to take into account the negative as well as positive impact of American culture. It is simply naive to lump it all together as a "product of freedom" that any sane person would indiscriminately embrace, as if the Bill of Rights or *The Sound of Music* and the misogynist lyrics that rap on about "bitches" and "hoes" ought to be somehow equal in the sights of the rest of the world.

Propriety and Civic Responsibility

For Hollywood's part, it would do well to heed some wisdom dispensed by Madeleine Albright. "I can totally understand that people in Karachi [a city in Pakistan] can be offended by the excesses of American mass culture," the former secretary of state says, "because they are in Kansas, too. I feel like an old fuddy-duddy saying this, but I understand this perfectly. I raised a family and can't tell you how many times I had to turn the TV off or change the channel when my girls were growing up."

What to do is something of a conundrum for a liberal society feeling its way into a future where information spreads everywhere nearly instantly. "We can't be in favor of censorship, of course," Albright continues. "What we're left with is a plea to the creators of entertainment that they must develop a sense of propriety. They have to develop a sense of civic responsibility—only with a global scope because that is the world we live in today." For an industry whose future relies on the global market, that is an economic as well as moral imperative.

The John Wayne-era assumption that America alone can write the script for the whole world has been forever foiled, both in Washington and Hollywood.

| "Hollywood is a global industry of movie producing networks that disobey most nationalizing criteria."

Hollywood Films Are Multinational Enterprises

Hans Erik Næss

Hans Erik Næss is a scholar in the Cultural Complexity in the New Norway program (CULCOM) at the University of Oslo, Norway. In the following viewpoint, he disputes the allegation that Hollywood cinema is purely an American product or synonymous with its culture. Including foreign investors, production companies, and directors, major American motion pictures are the product of transnational networks and parties, Næss asserts. Therefore, he claims that the European Union's battle against "American cultural imperialism," waged by providing additional support to the European film industry, will achieve limited success.

As you read, consider the following questions:

1. How does the author support his claim that Japan is a major presence in Hollywood?

Hans Erik Næss, "EU and the Global Hollywood," Eurozine.com, November 22, 2005. This article was first published in Norwegian in Le Monde diplomatique (Oslo) and has been provided by Eurozine. http://www.eurozine.com. © Hans Erik Næss, Eurozine. Reproduced by permission of Eurozine.

2. What big-budget American movies does the author list as being shot in Italy?

3. According to the author, why is "nationalizing" movies problematic?

Once more the European Union (EU) sets out to battle what is vaguely called "American cultural imperialism". Between 2007 and 2013, the EU will disburse 755 million euro to support the European audiovisual sector channelled through the programme known as MEDIA 2007. Its target is to "strengthen the audiovisual sector in Europe and let the movie production reflect European cultural identity and heritage".

If this campaign against Americanization is implemented without some profound adjustments, it will at best have limited success. The main reason is that EU policies regard American movies as synonymous to Hollywood and Hollywood as purely American.

But is that a problem? Yes, essentially because Hollywood is a global industry of movie producing networks that disobey most nationalizing criteria. At the end of the 1990s Japanese and European media conglomerates moved foreign financing for Hollywood movies to 70 percent.

One of the key reasons for this development is that the culture industry of today generates huge sums of capital. With the development of a more or less similar production structure as in other businesses leading the economic globalisation, Hollywood has become an open invitation to diverse investors—even those usually situated far from the entertainment industry.

As Old as Hollywood Itself

The globalisation of Hollywood, though, is as old as Hollywood itself. The French production company Pathé Frères, founded by the Pathé brothers in the late nineteenth century and finance by the investor Jean Neyret and the French bank Crédit Lyonnais, dominated the US market for a long time, releasing between 50 and 70 percent of all new movies. In 1908, for instance, the company was selling twice as many movies in the U.S. as all the American companies put together.

After World War II, this development became more methodical. The Hollywood majors increased their number of movies made abroad from 19 in 1949 to 183 in 1969. In 1966 the American government even blocked a takeover attempt from Banque de Paris et de Pays-Bas for Columbia Pictures. It did not prevent Crédit Lyonnais, however—until 1982 a government-owned bank—from becoming one of the leading sources in financing several Hollywood blockbusters, amongst others *Platoon* (1986).

1989 represents a watershed. Sony bought Columbia Pictures, making *Newsweek* magazine place the Statue of Liberty dressed in a kimono (guided by the headline "Japan Invades Hollywood") on one of their covers. The following year, Japanese company Matsushita Electric Industries Co. took over MCA which included Universal Studios. Two years later, Crédit Lyonnais acquired MGM/United Artists, before Canadian company Seagram Co. Ltd. purchased 80 percent of MCA, including Universal, while Matsushita kept the last twenty percent. In 2000, the French company Vivendi bought Seagram, still including Universal, before the merger between the American NBC and French-American Vivendi Universal Entertainment created NBC Universal in 2004, where the American company General Electric owns 80 percent of the shares. In 2005, a consortium led by Sony acquired MGM/United Artists.

Meanwhile, together with the financial globalisation of Hollywood, more and more of the actual production was being outsourced from the US. In 1998, for instance, 139 of 308 so-called "Hollywood movies" were shot abroad and characterized by American authorities as "runaway productions". In simple terms, this means that the relocation of Hollywood productions was of such an extent that it was considered troublesome for the American economy. Adding the fact that these productions involved a large share of local labour—in *The Bourne Identity* (2002), shot in the Czech Republic, where the share was 80 percent, which is quite normal—it becomes increasingly difficult to identify these Hollywood productions as anything but transnational.

The Tip of the Iceberg

This is just the tip of the iceberg. Besides the mere production of the movies we find similar networks within the chains of distribution and marketing. A brief example might be Canal Plus. As Europe's largest pay-TV service, it is airing 400 movies per year, 300 of which are first-run. Despite the attempts from the French government—who also have ownership interests in Canal Plus together with Vivendi—on reversing what they perceive as American cultural imperialism, they allow Canal Plus to buy their way into the investment company Carolco and subsequently finance movies like *Basic Instinct* (1992).

It is also important to point out that this is not just a matter of powerful Hollywood conglomerates chasing new markets. In many ways this is an agreed development. Ben Goldsmith and Tom O'Regan write in *The Film Studio: Film Production in the Global Economy* that the global production industry is dependent on the friendliness of governments in order to sustain and develop the local infrastructure of film studios.

Italian film and television production facility Cinecittà on the outskirts of Rome is a good example. Among big-budget movies shot here are *Hudson Hawk* (1991), *Cliffhanger* (1993), *Daylight* (1996) and *Mission Impossible III* (2005). Cinecittà Holding SpA, the largest shareholder in Cinecittà Studios SpA (17.5 percent), is owned by the Italian government, the movie production company Movieauro Srl., Vittorio Cecchi Gori

The 2008 Oscars

For the first time since 1965, all four acting Oscars handed out Sunday [February 24, 2008] went to non-Americans: Britain's Tilda Swinton, Britain/Ireland's Daniel Day-Lewis, France's Marion Cotillard and Spain's Javier Bardem.

Plus, the awards for original song and score went to an Irishman, a Czech and an Italian. Awards such as art direction, costume and makeup also went to Europeans.

PR-inside.com, "Hollywood's Globalization," February 28, 2008. www.pr-inside.com.

(the owner of Italy's largest distribution and production company), and the Italian bank Efibanca.

Moreover, we must not forget the artistic dimensions of a globalizing Hollywood. In the book *The Director's Cut: Picturing Hollywood in the 21st Century*, American psychologist Stephan Littger has interviewed 21 "Hollywood directors". Since eight of them are non-Americans, EU's categorization of Hollywood in pure national-American terms even here appears out of focus.

Wolfgang Petersen, the German director responsible for epic dramas like *Troy* and *Poseidon*, says to Littger that "when you leave your country for Hollywood, they say 'Now he's a lost soul and it's all very American'. I think that's all complete bullshit. Simply look at my movies or movies of other European directors who work here: they bring their heritage and their upbringing all with them". Alejandro González Iñárritu, the Mexican director of *21 Grams* and *Babel*, has a different take on the nationality question: "You know, I just make movies. Just that. Not Mexican movies, not Japanese movies, just movies. I hate when people want to nationalize art. It's like saying to someone who is French and is a painter, 'Do you paint French?'"

Defining a Movie's Nationality

The very idea of nationalizing movies is in general confronted by a rising number of problems. As for Norwegian film we can illustrate this from various angles. When *Factotum*, directed by Bent Hamer, was to be shown at the movie festival in Cannes in 2005, it was labelled as a German production in the festival programme, as a Norwegian movie by the Norwegian press, and as an American independent movie in the U.S. In connection with *The Danish Poet*, the winner of an Oscar for Best Short Animation in 2007—by the way co-produced by Norwegian Mikrofilm AS and National Film Board of Canada—an intriguing question surfaced: "When will we have the chance to see the first Norwegian Oscar winner since *Kon-Tiki?*"

Famous actress Liv Ullmann, who is the narrator of *The Danish Poet*, commented that neither *The Danish Poet* nor *Kon-Tiki* in fact were "Norwegian" movies. Jan Erik Holst at the Norwegian Film Institute argued the opposite of Ullmann, and claimed there were two ways of defining a movie's nationality: by looking at the producer or the director, in addition to the financier. Yet, this does not necessarily simplify things at all. If we are to follow Holst's definitions, a blockbuster like *King Kong* (2005) becomes a New Zealand-American-French movie. And by visiting the Web page of the Norwegian Film Institute, we discover that *The Danish Poet* is listed as a Norwegian-Canadian movie.

More trouble occurs elsewhere. European Audiovisual Observatory, a non-profit public service institution within the legal framework of the Council of Europe working to gather relevant information on the audiovisual sector in Europe, demonstrate in a report with the intriguing title "Making and

Distribution of Movies in Europe: The Problem of Nationality" substantial variation in definitions of nationality within
Europe.

In other words as long as EU continues to equalize the
boundaries between nation-states and cultures, their cultural
policy stays highly inflexible. To legally maximize a share of
external financing (that is, non-European) as a premise for
support from i.e. the fund named Eurimages, is an infertile
strategy. Especially when the Hollywood majors are given the
opportunity to have their projects financed by European investors—and even get public funding as well, as Luc Besson
did with *The Fifth Element* (1997).

The Global Realities

Consequently, the EU should refocus its cultural policy to
match the global realities of present-day Hollywood productions. In a study asked for by the European Council, sociology
professor Tony Bennett suggested that the cultural visions of
EU had to make a cosmopolitan turn. Bennett's argument for
this was that EU's cultural outlook was based on a conservative idea of a pan-European cultural heritage where large parts
of contemporary cultural diversity in Europe were excluded.
Hence it was necessary to raise the question of whether this
vision of "Europeanness" was to be preserved or redefined.

Seen in light of EU's so far modestly successful anti-
Hollywood strategies, I believe that the latter alternative
emerge as the most progressive one. Instead of conserving the
idea of culture as something being tied to the nation-state, EU
has the opportunity to mould a cosmopolitan cultural policy.
Other studies following Bennett's tracks support this conclusion. The efforts of tackling Hollywood cannot rest on a po-
larization between EU and the US, but must be understood as
a matter of dealing with the relations linking different kinds
of transnational networks—economic, political and cultural.

Periodical Bibliography

The following articles have been selected to supplement the diverse views presented in this chapter.

Paul Bedard — "Smoking Out Ciggies in Movies," *U.S. News & World Report*, September 15, 2008.

Michael Cieply — "After Virginia Tech, Testing Limits of Movie Violence," *New York Times*, April 30, 2007.

Cineaste — "Speaking Documentary Truth to Power," Summer 2008.

Information Week — "Hollywood Blamed for Scientific Ignorance," August 15, 2007.

Marni Jackson — "Sleeping with the Movies: From First Dates to Film Fests, Cinema Remains a Most Intimate Experience," *Reader's Digest* (Canadian), September 2007.

Donovan Jacobs — "Creating Reel Change: Maybe a Single Film Can't Change the World, But Put a Social Action Campaign Behind It and You Have the Seeds of a Movement," *Sojourners Magazine*, November 2006.

Rebecca Winters Keegan — "Can a Film Change the World?" *Time*, March 17, 2008.

Terri Murray — "Holywood: How the Religious Right Is Reshaping the Movie Industry," *Tikkun*, January–February 2006.

John Pilger — "Who's Afraid of Michael Moore?" *New Statesman*, 22, 2007.

Gene Seymour — "Do the Right Thing: Minorities in Hollywood Deserve More Recognition," *Newsday*, February 25, 2007.

OPPOSING
VIEWPOINTS®
SERIES

CHAPTER 2

Are Film Ratings Effective?

Chapter Preface

In March 2007, *Variety* magazine reported that Dan Glickman, chairman of the Motion Picture Association of America (MPAA), was pushing for a new category of especially graphic or explicit films restricted to viewers age 18 and up, "hard R." Some commentators claim that the R rating blankets too wide a range of films. Furthermore, the stigma of NC-17 can spell box-office doom. Industry insiders contend that not only is promoting and marketing NC-17 rated films saddled with limitations, most movie theaters refuse to show features with the rating. And rental franchises like Blockbuster do not carry NC-17 titles. According to one distribution executive, "Many movies have tried to reinstate a level of validity to the NC-17 rating, but it's complicated. The rating does have a chilling effect on the marketplace." Since its creation in 1990, only about twenty films produced by major studios have been rated NC-17.

Hard R is a balancing act for the MPAA to better adjust their ratings system and address the NC-17 dilemma, which had replaced the similarly problematic "X" rating. "Torture porn" films such as *Hostel* and the *Saw* series are examples of hard Rs. The video game-based *Hitman* and an edited version of *Zack and Miri Make a Porno* have recently earned the rating. Nonetheless, skeptics insist that hard R is not the solution. "If stores like Wal-Mart won't carry NC-17 DVDs," states entertainment site Wild Bluff Media, "what makes you think that they will carry hard R? [Our] bet is that instead of banning NC-17 from their shelves, they'll just ban hard R instead . . . a much broader category than NC-17."

The proposed hard R rating reflects the MPAA's challenges of deeming what content is—and is not—appropriate for younger audiences. The PG-13 rating came to be out of such concerns. In the following chapter, the authors debate if the MPAA's ratings system is an effective guide for parents.

"The system is not intended to approve, disapprove or censor any film; it merely assigns a rating for guidance."

MPAA Ratings Are Effective

Motion Picture Association of America (MPAA)

Founded in 1922, the Motion Picture Association of America (MPAA) is the trade association of the American film industry. The MPAA states in the following viewpoint that its film ratings, as determined by the ratings board of the Classification and Rating Administration (CARA), are fair and accurate. The rating system represents the diverse views of Americans nationwide, informs moviegoers of content and themes that may be unsuitable for children, and mirrors contemporary and changing parental attitudes, explains the MPAA. Furthermore, the association maintains that it does not aim to approve or censor any movie, leaving parents the responsibility to decide which movies their children should watch.

As you read, consider the following questions:

1. What "thematic elements" may raise a warning to parents, according to the MPAA?

2. How does the association respond to the question of why children are seen at R-rated movies?

3. In the MPAA's view, why does the ratings board operate in confidentiality?

The ratings of motion pictures are determined by the rating board of the Classification and Rating Administration ("CARA"), which includes a chairperson, a vice-chair, several senior raters and additional raters who all participate in the rating of individual motion pictures. The ratings are based on the level of certain content in the motion picture in order to provide parents with information to help them determine each film's suitability for viewing by their children. CARA attempts to select a diverse group of raters who represent the diversity of American parents such as parents from different parts of the country, including small towns and big cities. Each member of the rating board is a parent and has no affiliation with the entertainment industry outside their employment with CARA.

What happens if a filmmaker doesn't agree with your rating?

If the producer or distributor of the motion picture disagrees with the rating assigned to the motion picture, they have an opportunity to appeal the rating and argue that a lower rating should be assigned to the film. That appeal is heard by the Classification and Rating Appeals Board, which is made up of distributors and exhibitors knowledgeable about the industry. The Appeals Board determines whether the Rating Board's rating decision was clearly incorrect. This determination is made by considering whether or not a majority of American parents would concur with the Rating Board's finding. Also, the filmmaker can edit and resubmit the picture to obtain a lower rating than the one originally assigned by CARA.

How do you determine what puts a movie in one rating category over another?

A motion picture is evaluated in its entirety. The raters who view the entire completed motion picture will determine the most important factors that parents consider when deciding whether to allow their children to view that motion picture. The main considerations include the intensity of the themes in the motion picture, language, depictions of violence, nudity, sensuality, depictions of sexual activity and drug use. Motion pictures with adult themes or which include strong violence-, sexual- or drug-related elements will be rated accordingly to inform parents of those elements which may make the motion picture inappropriate for viewing by their younger children.

Rating Reasons

How do I know specifically what kind of material is in a movie?

Every motion picture rated PG, PG-13, R or NC-17 will be assigned "rating reasons" by CARA at the time that the motion picture is rated. These rating reasons provide additional guidance concerning the specific content of the motion picture and also give a further explanation of why the motion picture has been rated in the category to which it is assigned. The rating reasons also include modifiers to give parents an indication of the strength of specific elements in the movie. These rating reasons can be found in certain advertising of the motion picture in the rating box under the rating description. You can also find the rating reasons for any rated motion picture on www.filmratings.com. Some examples of rating reasons may include: "Rated R for strong violent images and some sensuality" (because language is not included in this rating reason, it means that the language contained in the movie was not at an "R" level); "Rated PG-13 for sci-fi action/ violence, some sexuality and brief language" (modifiers such as "some" and "brief" guide parents as to the level of those elements in the film). We encourage parents to get as much information as possible about the content of movies that their children may want to watch. That is why we have partnered with groups like Pause, Parent, Play, a clearing house for ratings information that parents can access on the Web at www-.pauseparentplay.org.

I have noticed "thematic elements" in the rating reasons—what does that mean?

Thematic elements are those elements of a film that do not necessarily fit into the traditional categories such as violence, sex, drug use and language, but may be of particular concern to parents. This rating reason raises a warning to parents to learn more about a film before they allow their children to view it. These thematic elements may include death, coming-of-age issues, verbal abuse, illness, abortion, and other serious subjects or mature discussions that some parents feel may not be appropriate for their young children.

Who decides what I see in a trailer?

Trailers and other advertisements for a movie are made by the company that produced or distributed the film in order to promote that movie. For all movies that have been or will be rated by CARA, the MPAA's Advertising Administration, a separate body, reviews all promotional advertising to ensure that: a) it does not mislead parents or consumers as to the proper rating for the motion pictures, b) the material included in the advertisement is suitable for the audiences who will be viewing it, and c) the rating of the motion picture and other relevant information is included in the advertisement.

The Rating System Is a Flexible One

Why does it seem that when I see movies from 10 or 20 years ago some material that was O.K. then is given a higher rating today and, on the other hand, other material is not rated as strongly?

The rating system is a flexible one, meant to consider parental attitudes at the time the motion picture is rated. The raters attempt, as much as possible, to mirror the views of a

A Magnet for Controversy

Her position as Hollywood gatekeeper—Joan Eldridge Graves ... has been with the Classification and Rating Administration since 1988 and its chair since 2000—puts her in the crosshairs of many culture wars. Are kids being oversexualized, and at younger and younger ages? Are they being desensitized by exposure to graphic violence? ...

Her job is a magnet for controversy, and Graves reacts to criticism by emphasizing two points. First, ratings are not intended as judgments on the merit of films. The board provides an informational service to parents that describes the content a film contains. Second, the raters strive merely to reflect the current sensitivities of American parents. Ratings are not proscriptive; hers is not a job of censorship.

Sonja Bolle,
"Discretion Adviser," Stanford Magazine,
July-August 2008. www.stanfordalumni.org.

contemporary cross-section of parents in the country. Thus, you may notice, for example, that as the concerns of parents about teen drug use or sexual activity increase, motion pictures which contain elements of illicit drug abuse or strong sexual content will be assigned a higher rating, reflecting the views of American parents.

Is cartoon violence assessed differently than realistic violence?

In reviewing a movie, the Rating Board will seek to assign the rating that most American parents would assign that same movie, keeping in mind various factors, including the level of violence. The realism of the violence may be one of the considerations. However, simply because a motion picture is animated does not mean that it is appropriate for children of any age. In fact, animated motion pictures have been assigned ratings from G to NC-17.

Why do I see children in the theater for movies that are rated R?

The R rating means that any child under the age of 17 may be allowed into the movie only if he/she will be viewing the movie with his/her parent or adult guardian. A movie that is rated R means that the rating board believes that the picture contains adult material, and signifies to parents that they should find out more about the film before they allow their children to accompany them to the film. The rating is a strong warning to parents concerning the language, violence, sexual content or other elements of the film, and indicates that it is not appropriate for young children. However, the decision of whether or not to bring their children with them to the R rated movie is left to parents.

Are the TV ratings the same as the movie ratings?

The G, PG, PG-13, R and NC-17 ratings were established for rating motion pictures and may only be used in connection with motion pictures that have been rated by CARA. Other entertainment, such as television shows and video games, are rated by other entities, with different rating designations, also in an effort to provide parents information about those entertainment media that may be viewed by their children. While the goals are similar, the ratings used for movies are not, and may not be, used for anything other than motion pictures rated by CARA. . . .

CARA's Work Is Confidential and Focused

Why doesn't CARA talk to the press about motion pictures that it rates?

The purpose of CARA is to provide parents with information about the level of content in a particular motion picture. CARA issues ratings and rating reasons for motion pictures to further that purpose. Once a movie is rated, CARA sends notification of that rating and the rating reasons to the public and the press to ensure it reaches parents. To safeguard the integrity of the rating process, discussions held by the Rating Board concerning a motion picture are confidential. The necessity for confidentiality is driven by the concern to protect the creative product of the submitter and to ensure that raters are not subject to outside influences in assessing the rating of a film.

CARA does provide explanations to the submitter of each motion picture of the reasons for the rating assigned to that picture. However, any such discussions concerning a particular motion picture will be only with the submitter and are also considered confidential. Thus, the substance of discussions about a movie being rated by CARA cannot be discussed with the press or anyone else other than, where appropriate, the submitter of the particular motion picture. The Chairperson of CARA speaks about the rating system with parents' organizations, industry groups and the press to promote a better understanding of the rating system by parents, the general public and members of the movie industry.

Do the ratings indicate if a movie is good or bad?

No, the system is not designed to serve the function of "critic." As the saying goes, PG does not mean "Pretty Good" and R does not mean "Rotten." The ratings do not determine or reflect whether a film is "good" or "bad." The system is not intended to approve, disapprove or censor any film; it merely assigns a rating for guidance—leaving the decision-making responsibilities about whether children should see the film to their parents.

Why doesn't CARA release the names of its raters?

Other than the chairperson, the vice-chair and the senior raters, the names of the members of the Rating Board are not provided to the public or any producer or distributor submitting a motion picture for rating. The reason for maintaining the confidentiality of their identities is to avoid even the appearance that they may be subject to outside influences.

> "*Parents are frustrated with a ratings system that ... is still used as a marketing ploy by many studios that release films cut to the very highest limits of the PG-13 or R-rating.*"

MPAA Ratings Are Not Effective

Rod Gustafson

In the following viewpoint, Rod Gustafson argues that the Motion Picture Association of America (MPAA) rating system does not effectively serve the interests of parents. He claims that the MPAA is submitting to pressure from independent filmmakers to persuade the movie business to embrace the NC-17 rating. The author contends that releasing more NC-17 films is a serious concern because theaters do not adequately enforce existing age and adult-accompaniment restrictions. Moreover, Gustafson states that the MPAA may eventually allow more sexually explicit and graphic content in rated-R films. The author is founder and senior reviewer of Parent Previews, *an online family-oriented entertainment guide.*

As you read, consider the following questions:

1. How does the author describe the PG-13 rating?
2. What is the author's view of the impact of sexually explicit and violent media on children?
3. In Gustafson's opinion, why is holding theaters accountable for enforcing age and adult accompaniment restrictions not an answer to the arrival of more NC-17 films?

With the recent media coverage regarding television ratings, few have taken notice of the other major media rating system that is being modified. The Motion Picture Association of America's (MPAA) movie rating system is about to be affected by subtle changes that I feel could spell big differences in the types of movies you find at your local theater. Perhaps even more interesting, these changes in a system intended to help parents are not due to pressure from moms and dads who are frustrated with using the ratings, but instead the catalyst is coming from filmmakers—especially independent producers.

But first, time for a short history lesson (a usual ingredient in my articles about movie ratings)....

For years, independent films were a rarity in the movie industry. The big studios—20th Century Fox, Disney, Columbia, Universal, Warner Brothers, and Paramount—were the rulers. They controlled virtually every aspect of moviemaking, and even issues they couldn't directly manage they would use their huge circle of influence to maintain or enact change in their favor. One of the ways they are able to exert this influential force is through the MPAA, an organization formed and operated by these six major players.

However, over past years, the technology required to make a movie has become far cheaper, and a huge surge of independents are cranking out films faster than ever before. Each January the Sundance Film Festival becomes *The Place* for indies [independent filmmakers] to show their wares and attract distributors (who are often owned by the big studios noted earlier) who will buy their films and then take them to market.

The Cinema Bureaucracy

But the road to getting a movie on a screen near you is riddled with various obstacles—one being the necessity to have the movie rated. There is no law in the United States that says a movie must have a rating (there is also no law requiring theaters to enforce the ratings), but one of the organizations falling under the MPAA's influential circle is the National Association of Theater Owners (NATO). This group works closely with the MPAA, and insists that any movies showing at a member's theater must have been rated by the MPAA Classification and Ratings Administration (one more acronym . . . CARA).

For an independent producer, that means he or she must have the movie rated or be satisfied with only showing it in independent theaters that are not part of NATO—usually "art house" screens often located in, shall we say, the less accessible parts of your community. Obviously, if you are hoping to make money from a movie you have made, you will want it playing in the giant multiplexes dotting America's suburbia.

Likewise, if one of the distributors owned by the big six studios is interested in your film, they will insist that you need to have a rating attached to the movie, as they are direct members of the MPAA.

At this point, a logical question would be, "What's the big deal? Why wouldn't you want to have a rating for your movie?"

It's no secret that most independent movies aren't likely to earn a G or even PG-13 rating. For that matter, the majority fall into the R-rated category and a significant number—upon their first submission to CARA—receive the even more restrictive NC-17 rating.

The Box-Office "Sweet Spot"

Movie marketers know the PG-13 rating is the box office "sweet spot." PG-13, PG, and G impose no age restrictions at the box office. They are merely "advisories" as to the content in the film. If a six-year-old can get to a theater, he can walk right in to a PG-13 film.

Thus, from a money-making perspective, the PG-13 rating is the perfect mix. It allows every age access to a film, but still subtly says to teen and adult patrons that there is some edgy content. However, an R-rating requires anyone under the age of 17 to be accompanied by a parent or legal guardian. (Although I'm certain it's unlikely anyone is asking for proof of guardianship at the box office.) Progressing further, an NC-17 film is not to be seen by anyone 17 or under. These restrictions can severely limit the amount of money your film will make, as teens form a huge part of movie audiences. But an even greater limiting factor exists, and for the most part is still outside the MPAA's circle of influence.

The owners of the buildings where these theaters reside, which are typically in shopping malls or similar developments, will often dictate that NC-17 movies cannot be shown on the premises. Other complications include newspapers and television stations that will not accept advertising for NC-17 movies. Finally, some theater owners simply don't think NC-17 movies are good for their business.

There's no doubt that getting an NC-17 movie to the marketplace is difficult, and that's where the issue of ratings is heating up.

More NC-17 Movies Are Coming to a Theater Near You

For years, independent producers (and foreign filmmakers) have claimed their movies receive stricter ratings than movies coming from the big six studios that contain similar content. One filmmaker who decided to make a strong statement about this inequality is Kirby Dick. His recent documentary, *This Film Is Not Yet Rated*, made its debut appearance at the Sundance Film Festival early [2006], and circulated through art house theaters [in the fall of 2006].

Dick also contests that sexual content is rated more restrictively by CARA than is violence, and that sexual behavior seen as (quoting Mary Harron, the director of *American Psycho* who is interviewed in the film) "unusual forms of sex" are especially prone to receive a higher rating.

This Film Is Not Yet Rated received an NC-17 rating for the graphic sexual examples he includes from other films. Yet, it's obvious that Dick only submitted the film for a rating to make his point and gain access to the inner workings of CARA. Dick then surrendered his rating, made revisions to the film to include the rating process he went through (which obviously wasn't included in the version originally submitted to the MPAA) and then released it as an unrated movie.

On January 23, 2007, *This Film is Not Yet Rated* releases to DVD, and the timing is impeccable, with the head of the MPAA, Dan Glickman, visiting the Sundance Film Festival in Park City, Utah and giving the producers there a big sense of hope for marketing edgier entertainment.

Kicking Off a "Campaign"

In the industry trade publication *Daily Variety* on January 16, 2007, it was reported that Glickman and ratings head Joan Graves would both be kicking off a "campaign" to help indie filmmakers and parents better understand the ratings system and make it more transparent.

His inspiration for making the changes? Dick's documentary.

Quoting Glickman directly from the article by *Daily Variety* writer Pamela McClintock: "The documentary made it clear that we probably haven't done as much as we can to explain how it all works," Glickman told *Daily Variety* adding that the voluntary ratings system—devised and implemented by Jack Valenti, his predecessor—is a "gem," even if it needs some polishing.

But on January 22, 2007, *Variety's* Web publication *variety .com* reported the results of the "kickoff": Glickman wants the movie business to embrace the NC-17 rating and has appointed a liaison to help filmmakers with questions about the ratings process. This is an obvious reaction to one of Kirby Dick's repeated points in his documentary is that no one knows who actually decides the rating of a movie at the MPAA. The names of the members of CARA's review board have always been secret, and filmmakers often receive conflicting reasons as to why a movie receives a particular rating.

But even more enticing to independent filmmakers working in edgy themes is Glickman's statement, "We are going to talk about this with the Directors Guild of America and NATO. [NC-17] is one of our ratings, and we would like to see it used more."

I'm betting this doesn't mean Glickman is going to instruct the board to issue more NC-17 ratings for movies that would now be rated R. That's further confirmed with another announcement he makes that explains how the ratings board will be using a new ratings descriptor to indicate certain R-rated movies aren't appropriate for younger children: (Hold that thought for a few paragraphs. . . .)

The Effects of Embracing NC-17

How this affects you will depend on where you sit with all of these variables. Some families are more sensitive to sexual content than violence. Others are the opposite.

However, I see problems with these changes, which should concern every parent, no matter which side of the sex versus violence fence you sit on.

To begin, if we are looking forward to the prospect of having more NC-17 movies playing in our neighborhood theaters, NATO better be prepared to do a far more effective job of checking for age verification than has been done in the past. In December 2001, the Federal Trade Commission's *Marketing Violent Entertainment to Children: A One-Year Follow-Up Review* . . . indicated that a study conducted for the report witnessed one-third of 13-year-olds and nearly two-thirds (62%) of sixteen-year-olds gained admittance to R-rated films without an accompanying adult.

This was just twelve months after the feds rattled the cages of the entertainment industry, threatening legislation-backed movie ratings if the MPAA's voluntary system could not be effectively enforced. Can we assume these compliance rates have improved any since then?

NC-17 films contain very high levels of sexual and violent content. It is probable to conclude a child or even teen could suffer psychological consequences after viewing such material. (I would suggest even many R-rated films have the potential to cause emotional harm to young viewers.)

Remember, unlike the bar on the corner of your street, there is no law you can fall back on if a slack theater employee doesn't check your child for age. There is no law forcing theaters to hire extra staff to make sure a teen who buys a ticket to a Disney film isn't heading for another cinema within a multiplex.

Further, if NC-17 movies are to become financially viable, they will need to be marketed somewhere. Outdoor advertising? Television? The Internet? Movie trailers at the start of other films? Will the industry be able to police itself in these areas?

Finally, back to my earlier comment regarding the decision to qualify certain R-rated movies as not being appropriate for young children. What does that mean? Isn't that inherently obvious in the R-rating itself? Or is this indicative of plans for the MPAA and CARA to acquiesce on certain films with more explicit sexual content, and give them an R-rating with this new descriptor instead of an NC-17 in order to balance the perceived inequality between sexual and violent content? It's important to recognize that R-rated films with this new descriptor will still allow *any* age patron into the film, as long as an adult accompanies them.

A Very Unhappy Ending

I can't help but feel as studios and independent producers fight this battle through the MPAA, that parents are on the outside of the loop. I fully endorse First Amendment rights, and recognize that those who want to produce NC-17 films have a right to do so. Yet children have rights as well, and it's up to adults to ensure their protection. The tobacco and alcohol industries have had to live with highly restrictive marketing and selling rules because their products are known to cause harm to children (and, arguably, adults). However, well over a thousand studies have concluded that violent media can have a detrimental impact on a child's mental health. Unfortunately, hardly any studies involving extreme sexual content have been completed, so we lack the scientific proof of potential harm.

Obviously, the answer is to make theaters as accountable as bars and retailers selling alcohol and tobacco. However, based on previous performance, I find it difficult to believe that theaters have the staff and resources to effectively limit access to minors from seeing these films, especially considering how many of their staff are minors themselves! And I'm certain these movies won't be exclusively promoted in "adult" media or in places where children won't be regularly seeing the advertisements.

I encourage parents to contact the MPAA and NATO and let them know they are being watched. The movie industry is already at risk of alienating a huge segment of their potential audience who write to me frequently complaining about not being able to find a film that meets with their tastes. Parents are frustrated with a ratings system that, despite the MPAA's claims of being very successful, is still used as a marketing ploy by many studios that release films cut to the very highest limits of the PG-13 or R-rating.

Our film industry is an essential part of our culture, and has long been a pastime families have enjoyed, and for the most part financed. With the constant pressure to push the envelope and appeal to a particular segment, which I personally believe is a small fraction of our society, Hollywood is at risk of writing itself a very unhappy ending.

> "The trend toward more permissive MPAA movie ratings—known as ratings creep—has happened for years."

Violence, Sex, and Profanity in MPAA-Rated Movies Is Increasing

Steve Persall

Steve Persall is the movie critic for the St. Petersburg Times, *a Florida newspaper. According to Persall in the following viewpoint, the Motion Picture Association of America's (MPAA's) rating system is becoming more lenient. He argues that the level of violence and aggression has markedly risen in G- and PG-rated movies from previous years. And Persall claims that, when it comes to R-rated features, the MPAA describes violence, sexuality, profanity, and other adult elements in a vague or generic manner that does not do the job.*

As you read, consider the following questions:

1. As stated by the author, how does the violence in *The Jungle Book* compare to that of *Pulp Fiction* and *Natural Born Killers?*

2. In the MPAA's words, what may be present in PG-13 movies, according to Persall?

3. In Persall's opinion, which rated-R descriptions are vague or generic?

I t's amusing that some parents are concerned about *Star Wars: Episode III—Revenge of the Sith* receiving a PG-13 rating for several violent scenes. They're upset that George Lucas added gruesome injuries, decapitations, even murdered children to his previously PG-wholesome saga, overlooking amputated hands in *Episodes V* and *II*.

As if Anakin Skywalker would become ruthless Darth Vader by peaceful means.

Where were these complaining parents for the past decade, when film violence in PG and PG-13 movies—along with profanity and sexual content—escalated to a level formerly reserved for R-rated movies?

Maybe it takes a cultural phenomenon like *Star Wars* displaying such a dark side for parents to notice.

But the trend toward more permissive MPAA movie ratings—known as ratings creep—has happened for years. A recent study by the UCLA [University of California, Los Angeles] School of Public Health on movie violence came to conclusions that are true today, based on a survey of films released in 1994, two years before the UCLA study began.

The Credibility Gap

Anyone who doesn't agree that movie content is generally more violent since then hasn't seen too many movies. The credibility gaps researchers pointed out in the MPAA's ratings system have only gotten wider.

"At the time we began, (the data) was current," said Lucille Jenkins, lead author of the UCLA report. "This is one of a few papers we've written on that research.

"Over 11 years, the MPAA hasn't changed any of its process, in terms of the ratings. It hasn't added any child-development specialists to the (ratings) board, hasn't added any new types of ratings, like a PG-16 or PG-18. We feel that the sample is representative of the same issues as today."

The UCLA study focused on the top-100 grossing films of 1994, except for Disney's animated, G-rated *The Lion King* and *The Madness of King George*, which was an unrated release. Violent acts were divided into three levels of intensity, from mild events such as shoving and slapping, to nonlethal aggression such as gunfire that doesn't kill, to graphic deadly force. Only three films—*Disclosure* (R), *Quiz Show* and *Reality Bites* (both PG-13)—didn't contain an act of violence.

The 1994 film with the highest-charted number of violent behaviors was *Timecop* starring Jean-Claude van Damme, with 110. Coming in third was Arnold Schwarzenegger's *True Lies* with 91. Both are rated R, but it's the second-place finisher that tipped off researchers about something in the MPAA system failing.

Disney's live-action version of *The Jungle Book*, runner-up with 97 violent acts, is rated PG, allowing unchallenged access while suggesting to parents that "some material may not be suitable for children." That's more mayhem than even *Pulp Fiction* and *Natural Born Killers*, released the same year with R ratings. Certainly Quentin Tarantino's imagination differs from Rudyard Kipling's, but the comparative frequency of aggression in *The Jungle Book* is surprising.

Breaking Down the Ratings

Even the infrequency of violence in some PG and R films in 1994 is remarkable. Both ratings categories contained at least one movie featuring only one violent act.

"I don't think we're telling them anything that they didn't already know," said Jenkins. "It's just that we have the science

The Effects of Animated Films

For G-rated films, our finding that animated films received significantly higher scores for violence than non-animated films suggests the need for additional research on the effects of animation on perception, particularly for young children. Given the possibility of long-term fear and anxieties from children's exposure to media, physicians should discuss media consumption with parents of young children and the fact that animation does not guarantee appropriate content for children. Researchers should make it a priority to explore the cognitive effects of films on children of different levels of development and to expand on the limited research that now exists about children's ability to distinguish reality from fantasy, while recognizing that understanding that something is not real does not necessarily negate effects.

Kimberly M. Thompson and Fumie Yokota,
"Violence, Sex, and Profanity in Films:
Correlation of Movie Ratings with Content,"
Medscape General Medicine, *vol. 6, no. 3, 2004.*
www.kidsrisk.harvard.edu.

now to back it up. Maybe that's why nobody (in the film industry) is jumping up and attacking (the findings) in any way."

So, where does the MPAA draw its nebulous lines? Objectionable language is obviously important, with the MPAA's rating descriptions noting that more times than any other factor in 1994's PG-rated films. Profanity was the second-most noted factor among R ratings, after violence. The UCLA study suggests that MPAA ratings are decided more often by what isn't in a movie, rather than what is.

Using the MPAA's own words from its Web site (www.mpaa.org) a PG rating is given to films in which "explicit sex scenes and scenes of drug use are absent; nudity, if present, is seen only briefly; horror and violence do not exceed moderate levels."

Meanwhile, PG-13 ratings can go to films in which "rough or persistent violence is absent; sexually oriented nudity is generally absent; some scenes of drug use may be seen; one use of the harsher sexually derived words may be heard."

When the MPAA describes R-rated content, the qualifications become vague, focused on "use of language, theme, violence, sex or . . . portrayal of drug use." In essence, the MPAA's definition of R-rated material can fit inside PG-13 qualifications. Only the frequency and severity of those factors lead to an R, and only a group of between eight and 13 ratings board members, many of them parents, decides how much is too much for PG and PG-13 standards.

Vague, Generic Rating Descriptions

Look closely at the MPAA's descriptions and ask a few questions. What exactly are the "moderate levels" of violence allowed in PG films? How brief can nudity be before it's unsuitable for a PG? What does "generally absent" mean with regard to nudity in PG-13 films? And what's the difference between drug abuses depicted in PG-13 films compared with R-rated movies?

Those vague, generic rating descriptions seen in movie ads and posters only tell us there's material in the movie that could be objectionable. They don't employ detailed descriptions of what kind of violence, profanity, drugs, nudity or sex are involved. Some rating descriptions for PG-13 horror movies are scarier than R descriptions. Using the qualifying terms "some," "brief" and "strong" don't do the job.

The UCLA study concludes that a quantitative measure of objectionable material should be initiated by the MPAA. Give parents an accurate count of how many objectionable acts are included in films, and a more precise description of what kind of acts they are. How graphic is the violence, sex and profanity? How often do they occur?

"We're not attacking the MPAA; we'd like to come across as an ally," said Jenkins. "My fingers are crossed that they would ask an outside organization to do a quantitative analysis, similar to what we did. They can hire somebody to watch the films, record the number of (violent) acts, record what we term the seriousness of those acts.

"As they sit down to discuss the films, they would at least have a consistent measure, some sort of number system that would be a little more concrete."

The more parents know, the more likely they'll make decisions to benefit children, rather than expose them to such material and fret about it later.

But that's where the profit factor kicks in, as it usually does in Hollywood. The MPAA works for the studios making the movies, looking out for its best interests from Washington, D.C., to the local megaplex. Anything the MPAA does to shore up the rating system may adversely affect ticket sales. Making moviegoers smarter simply isn't profitable, whether it's tighter ratings or more truthful advertising.

"This is a tricky situation because (the MPAA) is considered a self-appointed watchdog agency," said Jenkins. "Any big industry that only evaluates itself, and is only monitored by itself, and doesn't have any external evaluation, is suspect."

| *"Indeed, looking at the larger picture, there is evidence that ratings have in some ways become* stricter *over time."*

Violence, Sex, and Profanity in MPAA-Rated Movies Has Remained the Same

Steven D. Greydanus

Steven D. Greydanus is a film critic for the National Catholic Register *and founder of* Decent Films Guide, *a Web site of movie reviews with a Christian perspective. In the following viewpoint, he counters research claiming that the rating system of the Motion Picture Association of America (MPAA) has become permissive of objectionable content. PG-13 is not the "new R," and instances of profanity and similar elements have not increased in these movies, Greydanus contends. Instead, he suggests that MPAA ratings have become more stringent in some aspects, and many movies from previous decades would receive higher ratings if released today.*

As you read, consider the following questions:

1. What objectional content does *Adventures in Babysitting* have, according to Greydanus?

2. How does Greydanus compare the PG-rated *The Santa Clause* to its G-rated sequel *The Santa Clause 2?*

3. What does the re-rating of the movies *Planet of the Apes, Romeo and Juliet, Psycho,* and *A Man Called Horse* show, according to the author?

It sounded like a classic case of ratings creep.

In 2002, according to a July 16 *Philadelphia Inquirer* story ("Film rating trend raises creepy issues"), Nell Minow, a.k.a. the "Movie Mom" and film critic for movies.yahoo.com, went to see the PG-13 rated *About a Boy.* At one point in the film, Hugh Grant used an adjectival form of what the MPAA [Motion Picture Association of America] calls "one of the harsher sexually-derived words," but is often referred to as "the f-word."

According to the *Inquirer* story, "It once was verboten to utter [the f-word] in a PG-13 film. Then, it was allowed once—as an expletive, not to describe the sexual act." Minow, knowing the one-use rule, thought, *That's it. I won't hear that again.* But then the adjective cropped up a second time.

"So, now the standard changes," Minow said. "Instead of one, you can do two. That's how it happens. It's incremental."

Maybe, maybe not. Consider this: All the way back in 1987, *Adventures in Babysitting* featured not one but two emphatic uses of the f-word, not as an adjective but as a (nonsexual) verb, in back-to-back lines of dialogue. It also featured drug references, adolescent boys ogling porn, crass sexual references, and young children in recurring life-threatening peril from mobsters.

And it got a PG-13. In 1987.

In fact, so far from the f-word being off-limits in a PG-13 film in the 1980s, back then you could actually use it and get away with a PG rating, both before the advent of PG-13 (*Sixteen Candles*) and after (*Big, Eight Men Out*).

"The 'one f-word' rule has been inconsistently applied," Minow agrees, "but it is one of the very few 'rules' the MPAA will admit to having and of course it is absurd on its face." Clearly, she's right. For one thing, saying that you can use the word only once is also an invitation to be sure to get it in once. Filmmakers stragetically position their single use for maximum dramatic or comic effect, as when Jim Carrey screams it into the camera in *Bruce Almighty*.

All the Rage

Still, absurdity is one thing, and ratings creep is another. But ratings creep, real or imagined, is all the rage in the wake of a recent study by Harvard Kids at Risk Project researchers Kimberly Thompson and Fumie Yokota, who claim that films of a given rating today include on average more objectionable content than similarly rated films [over] ten years ago.

The study has generated a flurry of media stories warning parents that PG-13 is the new R, PG is the new PG-13, and G is the new PG. And there's some truth to that. But good luck finding any stories that raise any critical questions about the authors' claims.

Many stories have reported head-to-head test cases of older and newer films that Thompson says illustrate "ratings creep." One such comparison involves the original 1994 PG-rated Tim Allen comedy *The Santa Clause* and the G-rated 2002 sequel *The Santa Clause 2*, which Thompson says is more violent than its predecessor. Does this prove "ratings creep"? Consider:

- While *The Santa Clause 2* does involve some slapstick violence, the original *Santa Clause* includes a crucial early scene in which the "real" Santa slips off a roof and apparently *dies*. This could be *much* more disturbing to children than, say, the sequel's climactic depiction of Scott and Fake Santa struggling for control of the airborne sleigh.

- Language in the PG-rated original film includes "hell" and several instances of "oh my God." The G-rated sequel has no objectionable language of this sort.

- The original film includes some mildly risqué lines, including references to sleeping "buck naked," "freezing my nubs [testicles] off," and "1-800-Spank-Me." In the G-rated sequel, a line about "going pee-pee" is about as risqué as dialogue gets.

- The original film includes potentially troubling themes, including marital estrangement, divorce, and the legitimizing of the broken family, which for many children could be more stressful than anything in the sequel. While the sequel deals with remarriage after divorce, the first film's postmarital snarkiness and the death throes of a family could easily be more difficult for children.

Opinions of the Media

In spite of this, many media sources [such as *USA Today*] uncritically repeated some version of the claim that, compared with the G-rated sequel, the PG-rated original has "less sex and nudity, violence, gore and profanity."

Not that Thompson herself seems to have said anything about sex, nudity, gore, or profanity in these films. Her concern was the violence, which she apparently considers to trump other issues from risqué language to postmarital snarkiness. As a parent, of course, Thompson has the prerogative of deciding what is or isn't appropriate for her own children. But that's hardly proof of "ratings creep." And this is one of *her own test cases* offered in interviews to illustrate her claims.

Thompson's apparent greater sensitivity to violence over sexuality or language also figures in another one of her test-case comparisons: *Forrest Gump*, which she considers a hard PG-13 for 1994, and *Minority Report*, a hard PG-13 for 2002.

On the face of it, this comparison makes no sense: Why put a tragicomedy head to head with a sci-fi action thriller? Why not compare two similar films?

True, Steven Spielberg got away with some pretty gruesome stuff in the PG-13 rated *Minority Report,* especially in connection with eyeballs. Then again, two decades earlier in a PG film he got away with a beating heart ripped out of a victim's chest, not to mention child slave labor. In fact, *Indiana Jones and the Temple of Doom* pushed the limits of PG so hard that, along with *Gremlins,* it helped bring about the creation of the PG-13 rating.

Unbalanced Comparisons

Yet the film Thompson chooses to compare *Minority Report* with is *Forrest Gump*—a film rated PG-13 largely for sexual content, not violence. Once again, Thompson seems less interested in illustrating ratings creep generally than in suggesting that modern films are more *violent* than their earlier counterparts. But pitting *Forrest Gump* against *Minority Report* hardly proves that, any more than pitting the violent PG *Temple of Doom* against, say, the very gentle PG-13 *Whale Rider* proves the opposite.

Thompson's special concern over violence seems to lead her to weigh all violence the same, whether slapstick, stylized, realistic, etc. Does this make sense? Should a graphic depiction of terrorists decapitating a hostage, say, be counted as equivalent to Aragorn slicing off orc-heads in *The Lord of the Rings?* How about Mace Windu swapping off Jango Fett's fully helmeted head with a light saber in *Star Wars: Episode II—Attack of the Clones?*

This tendency to equate all violence leads is also behind another much-reported one of Thompson's comparison cases: the R-rated *A Time to Kill* (1996) and the PG-13 *The Return of the King* (2003).

This comparison was challenged in one of the only articles anywhere to cast doubts on the study. In a July 14 [2004] article for TheCelebrityCafe.com ("Harvard Study Shows Ratings Creep"), Internet writer Brian McCarthy points out, "*A Time to Kill* dealt with child rape, gunning down unarmed men and racial hate crimes (brick throwing, burnings). Granted there was more killing of creatures in [*Lord of the Rings*], but, *A Time to Kill* is still more violent."

Stricter and Looser

None of this is to say that there isn't a real big-picture ratings-creep phenomenon at work. There probably is—along with counter-trends of ratings getting stricter in some areas as well as looser in others.

Many older films, were they released today, would in all likelihood get a higher rating if released today. For example, movies with the f-word like *Big* and *Eight Men Out* could never get away with a PG rating today. Nor could you have a drug reference in a PG film, as *The Goonies* did in 1985.

Going back even further, a number of older films rated G that would never get that rating today, including the original *Planet of the Apes* (which includes much violence, menace, some disturbing imagery, and a prominent use of "damn") and Franco Zeffirelli's *Romeo and Juliet* (which shows the teenaged lovers naked in bed and ends with a double suicide). In fact, both of those G-rated movies were at a later date re-rated PG, proving that the ratings had gotten stricter. Likewise, some older films that originally received the equivalent of a PG rating, including *Psycho* and *A Man Called Horse*, were later re-rated R upon theatrical re-release or release to DVD.

The ratings creep phenomenon may well be real. However, anecdotal data offered by the study's authors are unconvincing.

The Study's Methods Raise Questions

What about the study itself? Where did the authors get their data? From a pair of parental content advisory Web sites, www.kidsinmind.com and www.screenit.com, which date to 1992 and 1994, respectively.

One thing this means, as the study's authors acknowledge, is that the study covers only the last decade or so, and their findings may not be reflective of the whole sweep of ratings history. Indeed, looking at the larger picture, there is evidence that ratings have in some ways become *stricter* over time as well as looser in others.

The study's use of parental advisory Web sites also raises other questions. Is data gathered from one Web site equivalent to that of the other? Have the reviewers always covered film content consistently over the years? Or might they have gotten better at their jobs with time, and provided more complete coverage of later films than earlier ones? The writers at *ScreenIt*, for example, acknowledge that in response to reader concerns they are more scrupulous today in documenting profanity in the proper religious sense of the term than when they first launched their site. So how uniform is the data?

What's the truth about ratings creep? Until we have a serious critique of the Harvard study, it's hard to say. Whatever the case, the Decent Films rule of thumb continues to apply: Parents shouldn't count on the MPAA system to do their job for them. No matter what the rating, parental guidance is *always* required.

Periodical Bibliography

The following articles have been selected to supplement the diverse views presented in this chapter.

Brooks Boliek	"A 'Hidden Film History' Unearthed: Movies Once Censored for Sex, Violence, and Race See Light," *Hollywood Reporter*, December 28, 2005.
Scott Bowles	"Debating the MPAA's Mission," *USA Today* April 10, 2007.
Richard Corliss	"Censoring the Movie Censors," *Time*, September 2, 2006.
Bruce Feirstein	"Nevermind PG, MPAA Goes P.G.! My New Ratings System," *New York Observer*, June 18, 2006.
Gloria Goodale	"Blood and Gore Find a New Venue: Movie Posters," *Christian Science Monitor*, April 13, 2007.
Rebecca Grace	"Why Parents Can't Trust Movie Ratings," *AFA Journal*, February 2007.
Mark Harris	"NC-17 Fatally Flawed," *Entertainment Weekly*, June 15, 2007.
Lauren Horwitch	"New Rules for the Ratings Game: The MPAA Makes Changes, Reaches Out to Indie Filmmakers," *Back Stage West*, February 22, 2007.
Laura MacInnis	"From G to R, Movie Ratings Have Gotten Absurd," *Miramichi Leader*, November 14, 2008.
Pamela McClintock	"Indecent Proposal: MPAA Working to Remove Stigma of NC-17," *Variety*, March 12, 2007.
Alan Mozes	"Many Kids Under 15 Watch Violent Movies," *U.S. News & World Report*, August 4, 2008.

CHAPTER 3

Is the Film Industry Appropriately Regulated?

Chapter Preface

According to Smoke Free Movies, nicotine on the silver screen is linked to 5,000 smoking-related deaths a month in the United States. The California-based advocacy group also maintains that 400,000 children light up for the first time each year because of such movie scenes. "Each time a member of the [film] industry releases another movie that depicts smoking, it does so with the full knowledge of the harm it will bring to children who watch it," Smoke Free Movies declares on its Web site, adding that the "tobacco industry has collaborated with Hollywood, including paid product placement." One solution the group proposes is that the Motion Picture Association of America (MPAA) ratings board automatically give R-ratings to movies that portray smoking.

However, the MPAA contends that portrayals of smoking are not rampant in movies. According to their research, of the 3,400 features released between 2003 and 2007, 57 percent contained smoking scenes, 75 percent of which were rated R. But in May 2007, the trade association announced that smoking would join strong language, nudity, and graphic violence as a criterion for ratings. "Clearly, smoking is increasingly an unacceptable behavior in our society," states Dan Glickman, MPAA chairman. "The appropriate response of the rating system is to give more information to parents on this issue." Declining the call for automatic R-ratings for movies that fail to kick the habit, advisories now include descriptions of "glamorized" or "pervasive" smoking.

While the role of smoking in movies has come under fire from Smoke Free Movies and other groups, regulation in Hollywood has always sparked controversy: The MPAA ratings system is voluntary and governed by a ratings board that has operated in secrecy until the last several years. In the following chapter, the authors offer their opinions on how effectively self-regulation serves the film industry.

> "Instead of restricting information with censorship, the [Motion Picture Association of America] would increase the available information, with classifications aimed at letting potential patrons know just what to expect."

MPAA Regulation Prevents Federal Censorship of the Film Industry

Jesse Walker

In the following viewpoint, Jesse Walker suggests that the Motion Picture Association of America's (MPAA's) film rating system—although inconsistent, mysterious, and sometimes oppressive—has kept federal censorship at bay. He claims that Frederic Howe and Jack Valenti, creator of the current MPAA ratings, acted as opponents against government restriction. Although Howe and Valenti played contradictory roles that both protected and suppressed free speech in film, a similar compromiser is now needed to fend off encroaching regulators, Walker states. Walker is the managing editor of Reason, *the magazine of the Reason Foundation, a Los Angeles, California-based think tank.*

Jesse Walker, "Censors for Free Speech," Reason.com, May 1, 2007. © 2007 Reason Magazine. All Rights Reserved. Reproduced by permission.

As you read, consider the following questions:

1. How did the film industry avoid the laws against impor-
   tation in 1916?
2. In the author's view, why were movie theaters shut
   down in 1908?
3. According to Jack Valenti, why did the National Association of Theater Owners oppose his original ratings proposal?

Jack Valenti, the long-reigning king of the Hollywood lobby-
ists, died [April 26, 2007], nearly four decades after he fa-
thered the Motion Picture Association of America's [MPAA's]
movie rating system. It is thanks to Valenti that compact codes
like "PG" and "NC-17" define who is allowed to watch a film
in a theater and who must wait 'til he's 18 or the picture
comes out on video, whichever happens first.

Semi-Voluntary Restrictions

From the beginning, the movies have faced not just direct
government censorship but unofficial, semi-voluntary restrictions by private bodies within the industry, formed to forestall
more intrusive regulations imposed from without. Three such
efforts stand out, each emerging during a period associated
with liberal reform. The National Board of Censorship, born
in 1909, was a product of the Progressive Era. The Production
Code Administration got its teeth in 1934, not coincidentally
the second year of the New Deal. And the modern MPAA ratings were created by a former aide to Lyndon Johnson in
1968, at the tail end of the Great Society. Each system was different from the others, but all embodied the same paradox:
They were formed to fend off public censorship, but it was
the threat of public censorship that gave them their power.

Movies did not initially enjoy the protection of the First
Amendment, and state and local governments almost immediately passed rules radically restricting what could be screened.

The U.S. Supreme Court ratified such sensorship in *Mutual Film Corp. v. Industrial Commission* (1915), declaring that "We would have to shut our eyes to the facts of the world to regard the precaution unreasonable or the legislation to effect it a mere wanton interference with personal liberty." Congress was more cautious about dipping its toes into content regulation, but it still managed to pass, for example, the Smith Act of 1912, which banned the transport of fight films across state lines. As early as 1916, members of the industry were adopting sometimes bizarre maneuvers to escape such edicts. In April of that year, a small party of entrepreneurs erected a tent on the boundary separating New York from Quebec. Over the course of five days, they projected a film of Jack Johnson's heavyweight fight against Jess Willard from one side of the border to the other, where it was rephotographed on American soil. During the procedure, the original negative was approximately one foot into Canadian territory; a customs official kept close watch to ensure that no one carrying it ever stepped onto U.S. soil. The idea was to import the images without actually importing the film—a clever, ridiculous, and ultimately doomed attempt to evade the Smith Act.

A Turning Point for the Film Industry

Rumors soon claimed that the effort had been an elaborate feint: not a way to import a movie so much as an alibi after the movie was found on American soil. If so, the process was even more revealing. To project a movie over a national frontier to avoid the law is odd enough, but to do it as a *cover story* is positively baroque.

And the Smith Act was relatively lenient. On Christmas Eve, 1908, New York Mayor George McClellan, Jr., the son of the Civil War general, shut down all the city's movie theaters. Theoretically this was a public health measure—the venues were denounced as dirty and cramped—but the real reason for the command was pressure from anti-movie moralists, from nativists who distrusted the theaters' immigrant audiences, and from vaudeville houses and other institutions that didn't like the competition. The mayor's decision was soon rescinded, but the prospect of losing the entire New York market rattled the movie business. So the Motion Picture Patents Company, a patent pool cure cartel that was the industry's most powerful player, allied itself with the People's Institute, a New York-based Progressive group. The result was the National Board of Censorship. The Progressives, the historian Nancy Rosenbloom wrote, "hoped to create better alternatives to saloons, dance halls and the streets" by "transforming the moving picture shows into cleaner, safer social centers and by encouraging the production of quality entertainment." To that end, they signed on to the new National Board, which soon became, paradoxically, both the chief censor of motion picture content and the chief force fighting legal censorship.

The Chief Spokesman for Free Speech

In more recent years, it seemed strange that when would-be censors attacked films they judged too erotic or violent, the chief spokesman for free speech would often be Valenti, the creator of a ratings system that routinely enforces repressive and inconsistent standards. But he was hardly the first man to play that contradictory role. For a period in the 1910s, Frederic Howe was simultaneously the chair of the National Board of Censorship and a vocal opponent of government censorship, helping to lead a legal fight against political interference in film content. If that wasn't confusing enough, Howe's most notorious conflict with the rest of the board came not because he judged the group too strict but because he thought it was being too lenient: He was upset that it had approved D.W. Griffith's pro-Klan epic *The Birth of a Nation*.

Independent filmmakers have long charged the MPAA with discriminating against movies made outside the major studios. In the Progressive Era, similarly, investigators accused

Jack Valenti Tries to Create Balance

It was plain that the old system of self-regulation, begun with the formation of the MPAA [Motion Picture Association of America] in 1922, had broken down.... From the very first day of my own succession to the MPAA President's office ... there was about this stern, forbidding catalogue of "Dos and Don'ts" the odious smell of censorship. I determined to junk it at the first opportune moment.

I knew that the mix of new social currents, the irresistible force of creators determined to make "their" films and the possible intrusion of government into the movie arena demanded my immediate action.

Jack Valenti, "How It All Began,"
MPAA.org, 2005. www.mpaa.org.

the National Board of colluding with the Patents Company to penalize pictures made by filmmakers outside the cartel. If the collusion was real, it ended in 1915, after an antitrust suit broke up the Patents Company. After that, the board's influence faded; it soon renamed itself the National Board of Review, and today it is known mostly for its annual film awards. Many movie critics wish they could be censors. These censors were reduced, or elevated, to the status of critic.

The feds imposed draconian controls during World War I—one filmmaker was actually imprisoned for making a movie about the American Revolution, on the grounds that it might "create a prejudice" against our ally Great Britain—but afterwards the crackdowns would return to the state and local levels. There [were] no effective nationwide restrictions on movie content until 1934, when the liberal Motion Picture Research

Council and the conservative Legion of Decency were both fanning calls for controls, Congress was considering several bipartisan censorship bills, and FDR's [Franklin Delano Roosevelt's] National Recovery Administration was imposing its own code on the industry, complete with content rules. In that environment, Hollywood rushed to create an internal enforcement body lest it have to answer to someone else. Henceforth, mainstream American filmmakers would have to obey a set of dos and don'ts in which "methods of crime shall not be explicitly presented," "sex perversion or any inference to it is forbidden," and "scenes of actual childbirth, in fact or in silhouette, are never to be presented." Films could not "throw ridicule on any religious faith," seduction was "never the proper subject for a comedy," and vengeance could not be justified "in modern times," though "in lands and ages of less developed civilization and moral principles, revenge may sometimes be presented."

The Freedom of Film Does Not Last

The code would remain in place until 1968, when Valenti's ratings supplanted it. But the commands started to lose their force after 1952, when the Supreme Court ruled in *Burstyn v. Wilson* that the First Amendment protects motion pictures after all. The decision revoked the regs imposed by state and local prudes and scaled back the threat of federal censorship; between that and changing social mores, filmmakers such as Alfred Hitchcock and Billy Wilder were soon getting away with material that never would have passed the censors in the '30s. By sweeping away the increasingly archaic Production Code, the MPAA ratings looked like a blow for free expression. Instead of restricting information with censorship, the judges would *increase* the available information, with classifications aimed at letting potential patrons know just what to expect.

It didn't work out that way. According to Valenti, the original proposal didn't include a rating stronger than R, but the National Association of Theater Owners objected, arguing that allowing minors to see extremely explicit films would leave the venues open to legal harassment. The result was the X rating, now called the NC-17, which before long was associated so closely with pornography that it became the kiss of death for any non-porn film that received it. The ratings, meanwhile, are imposed by a shadowy central authority with its own peculiar prejudices. Many filmmakers have questioned the workings of that mysterious council. In Kirby Dick's documentary *This Film Is Not Yet Rated*, for example, Matt Stone contrasts the treatment given his early film *Orgazmo*, released independently, and his later effort *South Park: Bigger, Longer, and Uncut*, released by a major studio. When the first cut of *Orgazmo* got an NC-17, he reports, the MPAA said it was "for the overall sexual content"; asked if there was any way to recut the picture to get an R, the association said they were welcome to submit a new version but "we don't give specific notes." With *South Park*, by contrast, Stone says the board "was extremely specific"—they were told to remove "this word, this line, this joke." When *Orgazmo* was released, it still had an NC-17. *South Park* went out with an R.

Repelling Formal Censorship

The MPAA has a lot of influence, but it can't really block an unrated film from theaters. It has become much less difficult, though hardly painless, to put out a movie without its stamp of approval, and even the big studios are happy to avoid their own rules when it comes time to call in those theatrical prints and issue an uncensored director's cut on DVD. But even as the system grows weaker, battered by the less-regulated alternatives of the Internet and home video, the drive to control what people can say and hear continues unabated. It merely shifts its focus to a different medium.

The day before Jack Valenti died, the Federal Communications Commission released a dubious report about violent television's alleged effects on children. It ended with a call for new regulations, and while those proposals are couched—like the movie ratings—in the language of consumer choice, it's hard to miss the authoritarian impulse that runs through the report. The government wants to *control what people see.* "Violent speech and depictions of violence have been found by the courts to be protected by the First Amendment," the commission concedes. But then it quotes the Supreme Court's 1978 [*Federal Communications Commission v.*] *Pacifica* decision, which noted that broadcasting receives "the most limited First Amendment protection." The report suggests, among other approaches, that Congress restrict violent programming to particular hours of the day. (The FCC [Federal Communications Commission], apparently unable to program its VCR, seems to assume the same is true of the country's children.) Members of Congress have gone further, speculating routinely about imposing the FCC's indecency rules on cable and satellite broadcasters. In the most radical proposals, pushed by [Senator] Ted Stevens (R-Alaska) and others, such controls would be extended even to premium channels such as HBO [Home Box Office], disrupting the creative freedom of *The Sopranos, The Wire, Deadwood,* and other landmark works of art that simply couldn't exist as either network TV shows or theatrical movies.

I don't expect that particular scenario to happen. But that doesn't mean there won't be any new encroachments on televised speech. As the regulators close in, the time will be ripe for a new Jack Valenti or Frederic Howe to emerge—a great compromiser who can repel formal censorship by extending the informal kind, its nominally voluntary nature belied by the guns of the government lurking behind it.

> *"If the MPAA is going to continue to oversee the ratings system, it must . . . disavow homophobic discrimination and place more restrictive guidelines on violence rather than sex."*

MPAA Regulation Censors the Film Industry

Kirby Dick

In the following viewpoint, Kirby Dick argues that the Motion Picture Association of America's (MPAA's) rating system is biased and censors independent and gay filmmakers. Dick maintains that, in secrecy, the MPAA skews its ratings to be lenient of violence and harsh on sexuality—especially homosexuality—to serve the interests of the six major Hollywood studios it represents and gain favor in Washington. Therefore, he calls for the trade association to make its ratings and appeals board public and balance its restrictions on violence and sex. Dick is an Academy Award-nominated filmmaker who directed the documentary on the MPAA's rating system, This Film Is Not Yet Rated.

As you read, consider the following questions:

1. How does Kirby counter the argument that the ratings board members require anonymity to shield them from outside influences?

2. How does Kirby's view of violent content differ from his view of sexual content?

3. What benefits has the MPAA gained by earning the favor of Washington conservatives, in the author's opinion?

The Motion Picture [Association] of America [MPAA] and the National Assn. of Theatre Owners [in January 2007] heralded a "reform" of their film ratings system, which assigns the ratings G, PG, PG-13, R and NC-17 to most films released in this country. Unfortunately, the MPAA's changes are almost entirely cosmetic and only go a small way toward fixing a broken system—a system so closed to public scrutiny that no news organization had been able to disclose its workings until they were revealed in the documentary *This Film Is Not Yet Rated*, which I directed.

Despite protestations to the contrary, it appears that the film shamed the MPAA into paying lip service to its critique. As the film revealed, the association has been violating its own rule that raters must have school-age children, and it has refused to allow filmmakers to refer to other films when they appealed a rating. Both absurdities will be fixed.

But these are minimal changes. All of the fundamental problems of the ratings system remain: its secrecy and lack of accountability, its bias against independent and gay filmmakers and its excessive concern with sexuality while rating violence much less restrictively.

For nearly 40 years, film ratings in the United States have been decided by a secret board. Although the MPAA now plans to announce the names of three of the 11 film raters, the majority will still be anonymous. [The names of three se-

The "Voluntary" Rating System

This [Motion Picture Association of America (MPAA)] rating system is "voluntary," and is allegedly designed to protect children from being corrupted by evil movies. By voluntary, of course, this means that if you want any major distributor to pick your film up, . . . any major theater chain to *play* your movie, . . . anyone under the age of 18 to see your movie at all at almost any theater in America, it has to be rated by the MPAA. But, of course, you don't have to get it rated if you don't want to.

*Justin Brown, "Movie Ratings Doled Out by
MPAA Trade Association Censor Artists,"
The Tartan, April 9, 2007. www.thetartan.org.*

nior raters were posted online.] The MPAA claims their names are withheld to protect the raters from influence. But there are many people in society who make important decisions—judges, school board officials—whose identities are not shielded. In fact, by knowing who is making these decisions, the public is better able to discover improper influence.

The MPAA also refuses to release the names of the members of its appeals board, which is the final arbiter in the ratings process. This is particularly troubling because the appeals board is almost exclusively made up of executives from corporations that belong to the MPAA or the theater owners association, the very corporations that stand to gain the most from influencing a rating.

A Conflict of Interest

The MPAA claims the ratings system is for the public. If it's truly for the public, it should *be* public.

Not surprisingly, conflict of interest is at the root of the problem. In addition to overseeing the ratings system, the MPAA is also the trade organization and lobbying arm of Hollywood's six major film studios, which collectively own more than 95% of the U.S. film business. This explains why studio films with excessive violence time and again receive unreasonably light ratings, granting them greater access to the highly coveted teenage audience. On the other hand, films made or distributed by the studios' competitors—independent and foreign film companies—which more often contain adult sexuality, are rated much more harshly, often receiving an NC-17 rating.

The ratings board does all of this in the name of "protecting children," even though most media experts believe that exposure to violent media is far more damaging to children than exposure to sexual media. In most of Western Europe, ratings systems are much more restrictive of violence than sex.

Even more disturbing, the ratings board, as my documentary clearly demonstrates, rates films with homosexual scenes much more restrictively than films with similarly shot scenes of heterosexuality. But the MPAA has refused to disavow its discrimination against films with gay content.

A Discriminatory Precedent

When asked in *This Film Is Not Yet Rated* why gay films were rated more restrictively, Kori Bernards, the MPAA's vice president of publicity, said that "we don't try to set the standards, we just try to reflect them."

This is appalling. If the MPAA thought that the country's standards were racist, would their ratings reflect that racism? If the standards were anti-Semitic, would the ratings reflect anti-Semitism?

The MPAA should be called on to publicly state that no film shall be rated more restrictively on the basis of the race, religion, ethnicity or sexual orientation of its characters.

Censorship of films with sexual content actually serves the MPAA's political interests in Washington. One of the MPAA's primary objectives is lobbying Congress to pass laws favorable to the film studios. By harshly rating films with sexual content, the MPAA has curried favor with conservatives in Congress who have rewarded them by passing a number of very onerous intellectual property laws that have added billions of dollars to film studios' coffers while greatly restricting the development of new art forms and new technologies.

An effective and unbiased film ratings system is of great importance to parents, educators, film audiences and filmmakers. If the MPAA is going to continue to oversee the ratings system, it must make some real changes: reveal the names of all members of the ratings and appeals board, disavow homophobic discrimination and place more restrictive guidelines on violence rather than sex. The sooner it makes these changes, the better.

> "Old staples such as compelling narratives and artful film-making are increasingly taking a back seat to the promotion of brands."

The Film Industry Has Become Over-Commercialized

Robin Good

In the following viewpoint, Robin Good claims that product placement and commercialism threaten film as an art form in mainstream cinema. He suggests that even though such practices have always been a part of the Hollywood film industry, they have reached extremes that interfere with the creative vision of directors and writers—to the degree that today's movies have become sanitized vehicles for advertising. As a result, the author believes that discerning audiences have begun to look elsewhere, especially the Internet, for authentic and inspired entertainment. Robin Good is a media analyst and founder of Master New Media, *a business and media online magazine.*

As you read, consider the following questions:

1. In the author's view, how are movie studios persuaded to participate in product placement?

2. According to the author, how has commercialism affected television and politics?

3. What similarity does Good view between product placement strategies and propaganda?

Product placement presents consumer products, brand names and locations to film and television production teams for inclusion in their projects. The goal is the one of raising brand awareness while selling the idea to movie production houses as a "clever" way to reduce their costs while providing greater "authenticity" to the environments and characters shown. [According to Wikipedia.org,]

> Product placement appears in plays, film, television series, music videos, video games and books, and is a relatively new idea (first appearing in the 1980's). Product placement occurs with the inclusion of a brand's logo, or a favorable mention or appearance of a product. This is done without disclosure, and under the premise that it is a natural part of the work. *Most major movie releases today contain product placements.*

Product Placement Is Mutually Cost-Effective

As a matter of fact, relative to the high cost of 'above the line' media, where both producing commercials and booking media space require huge money investments, product placement inside commercial films is a highly cost-effective way to gain huge exposure and visibility at a fraction of the traditional advertising costs.

Indeed, product placement inside movies have been around for at least as long as Hollywood has, but it never before has been as influential and powerful as it is now.

Old staples such as compelling narratives and artful filmmaking are increasingly taking a back seat to the promotion of brands, while many of the key creative decisions are gradually wrangled out of the director vision and handed over to the marketing people.

America, your movie-making dream machine is broken.

And with the Hollywood film-making in such a dire state, there is little wonder that audiences are rapidly turning their noses to Internet television, online video, to Open Source film-making and even to the newest game-inspired film-making craze, Machinima, to avoid the sanitized, hyper-commercialized fare being rolled out by Hollywood.

The saddest thing among these rampant practices, is that film audiences, especially American ones, are increasingly numb and unaware of the consequences and issues connected to such practices and voice little complaints and open critique to this ongoing creative slaughter.

Not All Viewers Are Blind to the Exploitation

Obviously, with some due exceptions:

The Media Education Foundation—or MEF—was set up to question our apathetic acceptance of these practices on the part of the mass media, producing a range of thought-provoking documentaries that challenge the media status quo.

> The Media Education Foundation produces and distributes video documentaries to encourage critical thinking and debate about the relationship between media ownership, commercial media content, and the democratic demand for free flows of information, diverse representations of ideas and people, and informed citizen participation.

As grassroots, people media emerge as a powerful alternative and competitor to traditional mainstream media, it becomes increasingly important to question the motives, assumptions and practices of the "old" media to avoid repeating the same mistakes.

Matt Soar and Susan Ericsson's film *Behind the Screens* attempts to tackle the issue of Hollywood hyper-commercialism and supplies a solid critique of current mass media marketing practices. . . .

Read on to see just how far product placement has permeated our culture.

Hollywood Parodies Its Own Greed

It is no secret, then, that product placement runs rampant through mainstream media and nowhere more so than in Hollywood cinema.

We know it, and apparently they know it.

And yet, somehow many among us still accept and actively finance with movie entrance tickets the production of such shallow movie content.

In this first [example], taken from the Hollywood movie *Wayne's World* we see Hollywood parodying its own greed.

Admittedly it's funny, but only because it strikes a raw nerve. In the average movie, we are subjected to as much product placement as we are character development, and often considerably more than that.

While Mike Myers is smart for taking a jab at the product placement machine, it is ultimately the studio that has the last laugh. There are no Duffs or Brand X products to be seen here—as we laugh at the blatant hyper-commercialism of Hollywood, so we are fed yet more blatant hyper-commercialism.

President George W. Bush Follows Suit

Hollywood is not alone, however. For while Hollywood might take the most flack, product placement has permeated every strata of society, from the commercialization of schools, to presidential speeches.

That's right—presidential speeches.

Now certainly advertising isn't necessarily a bad thing. The growth of online contextual advertising, for instance, has had a great impact in terms of bringing Web visitors integrated, non-invasive advertisements that are (at least some of the time) of interest to them.

Product placement is the antithesis of contextual advertising—it attempts to sneak in an entirely different agenda, shaping meaning into meaninglessness in an effort simply to push home its subliminal message. If this is unacceptable to movie goers, it should be even more so to political voters.

In this second brief [example] we see [former president] George W. Bush sliding a blatant bit of advertising into a public speaking engagement. Now certainly there are a good few more reasons not to trust Bush than this, but that's another story. What is amazing is that product placement has moved out of the movie theater and up onto the political podium. . . .

Hyper-Commercialism as a Way of Life

Advertising does not need to work this way. There are other evolving models that allow for a bottom-up, customized and credible approach to marketing.

But for as long as we accept this Hollywood staple gone wild, we will be subjected to pernicious, insidious, creeping product promotion at every turn.

In this final [example], which gathers highlights of the excellent exposé documentary *Behind the Screens*, we see how advertising serves as the driving force behind Hollywood movies, at the expense of entertainment.

The film blends actual footage of product promotion with sharp critique from screenwriters, critics and political economists. In this [example], it becomes glaringly apparent that:

- Hollywood has, in the last thirty years, entered a period of hyper-commercialism with much greater ties to marketing, advertising and product promotion

- *The methods of product placement are much the same as those of propaganda.* Through repetition and integration into everyday scenes, the unnatural or unnecessary is naturalized and made desirable

- *Even as far back as fifty years ago,* diamond companies were bribing script writers to promote the romantic connotations of the diamond engagement ring

- *However, early product placements were ad-hoc, whereas now they have become the norm,* impacting upon the entire production process of a film

- Filmmakers are enticed into branding gadgets and peripheral items in a bid to save money from their inflated budgets. The bigger the budget, the greater the need to offset its risk with the use of heavy product placement

- *Just as TV's integrity has suffered* at the hands of insidious omnipresent marketing, so film increasingly sacrifices all to make a quick buck

The Future of Film Art Is at Stake

Of one thing you can be sure: *For as long as we accept this diluted pseudo-entertainment,* Hollywood will continue to serve it up.

The best thing any of us can do is vote with our feet and with our wallets by stopping this endless funding of this blatant, unethical, uncaring and relentless corporate propaganda machine.

Media are becoming increasingly personal, and increasingly plausible for anyone to take up and get involved in. The days of mass audiences for mass media are quite clearly numbered, and if advertisers want to survive beyond the next decade, they are going to have to take advantage of new business models.

The engaged, discerning audiences of the evolving new media landscape will demand that this involves film-makers, reporters, videographers and other media makers being allowed to retain their autonomy and integrity.

For while many of us accept Hollywood's product placement as business as usual, Web audiences, who can pull and steer their viewing preferences with much greater control, are less forgiving, as we are going to increasingly witness in the coming years.

As Hollywood box office figures seem to hold steady figures for the last few years it is only up to you to vote with your choice whether you would like to continue seeing [these] practices expand and conquer what once was a space reserved for communicating insight, vision, philosophy and our own history.

There may be a good lesson to be learned here and a great opportunity to regain that credibility and value, that, at least in my eyes, Hollywood has long lost.

| "*Product placement is almost as old as moving pictures themselves.*"

The Level of Commercialism in the Film Industry Has Not Changed

Joanne Weintraub

Joanne Weintraub states in the following viewpoint that product placement and commercialism are Hollywood traditions. The author claims that arrangements between film studios and major corporations have existed since the first motion pictures of the 1890s. Weintraub explains that some critics tend to romanticize Hollywood's early years as free of such advertising ploys and partnerships, but as she points out, there is no doubt that product placement has existed in motion pictures since the beginning. Nonetheless, she casts doubt on the influence of product placement and brand promotion on moviegoers' buying habits. Weintraub is a television columnist for the Milwaukee Sentinel Journal.

As you read, consider the following questions:

1. How does Weintraub describe product placement in the 1920s?

2. In Weintraub's view, how does product placement differ between film and television?

3. How did students at Iowa State University's Greenlee School of Journalism and Communications describe movies and brand promotion, according to the author?

Most cable TV film festivals celebrate such familiar names as Hitchcock, Hepburn, Cukor or Cagney.

Turner Classic Movies' [TCM's] latest festival is built around names like Buick, Budweiser, Coca-Cola and Marlboro.

Product Placement in the Movies, which will run every Friday in March [2005], is a novel idea for an anthology of popular films.

It demonstrates that the "casting" of consumer products in on-screen roles didn't start with the conspicuous brand preferences of Austin Powers or James Bond, nor even with Steven Spielberg demonstrating the power of Reese's Pieces to attract a friendly extraterrestrial in 1982's *E.T.: The Extra-Terrestrial*.

The 11 films in the TCM anthology, dating from *Scarface* in 1932 to *Urban Cowboy* and *Superman II* in 1980, represent a small sampling of movies whose producers have, in effect, sold screen space to advertisers, sometimes for cash but more often in exchange for valuable goods or services.

From Nearly the First Reel

In fact, said media analyst Jay Newell of Iowa State University in Ames, product placement is almost as old as moving pictures themselves.

The Lumiere brothers, those famous French film pioneers of the 1890s, had an associate who also worked as a publicist for Lever Bros., now the international heavyweight known as Unilever.

It was not by accident, said Newell, that Lever's Sunlight Soap can be seen in several widely distributed Lumiere features as early as 1896.

"We tend to romanticize the past, and to think that art was purer then, or at least less commercial," said Newell, an assistant professor at Iowa State's Greenlee School of Journalism and Communication.

"But if (product placement) is a sin, it's an original sin. It's been a factor in movies from the very beginning."

Newell has been teaching advertising and mass communications at Iowa State since 2003. In an earlier life, he was director of on-air promotions for Turner Broadcasting's CNN [Cable News Network] and TNT [Turner Network Television] cable channels.

Newell, who has done extensive research on the history of product placement at the Academy of Motion Pictures Arts and Sciences archives in Hollywood, served as an adviser to TCM on the movie anthology.

"We always try to look at different angles of film and film history," said Charlie Tabesh, TCM's senior vice president of programming, "and this one intrigued me because it addresses head-on the balance between art and commerce in the movies."

The 1920s Started It All

According to Newell, the flirtation between movies and consumer goods blossomed into true romance in the late 1920s. That's when production files in the motion picture academy's archives begin to bristle with letters from publicists suggesting joint advertising campaigns.

Back then, "it was not about cash changing hands, it was about trading attention," Newell said.

If the product was a substantial one, like the Buick automobiles that made their way into many Warner Bros. movies in the 1930s, or even a railroad car or airplane, the freebie or loaner represented substantial savings for film producers.

But much more lucrative were advertising tie-ins—or "tie-ups," as they were then called.

White Owl Cigars, for instance, provided a then-generous $250,000 worth of advertising for the 1932 *Scarface* in exchange for the right to claim that star Paul Muni smoked them in the movie.

Chesterfield cigarettes had a similar deal with the producers of *You'll Never Get Rich*, a 1941 movie starring Fred Astaire.

In addition to its arrangement with Buick, Warner Bros. also had a long-term deal with General Electric to feature its newest refrigerators in kitchen scenes. Coca-Cola was "absolutely brilliant," said Newell, at negotiating the right to pass around Cokes during breaks in filming, then promoting both its own product and a movie such as 1933's *Dinner at Eight* with pictures of Jean Harlow and other glamorous stars swigging soda pop.

Just as canny, but more subtle, were the DeBeers diamond people, who worked through an advertising agency to promote their product in movies as the ultimate in romantic gifts—and, of course, an absolute necessity for a man to give to his new fiancee.

Networking with Bob Hope

Introducing each of the TCM films on the air will be George Simkowski, a veteran Chicago ad man who more or less stumbled into the product placement game more than 40 years ago and has been playing it ever since.

A Reflection of Reality

In some ways, the abundance of products in film ... is merely a reflection of reality. We are a society obsessed with brands. As I write this, I am in a Starbucks. I'm on a Mac with the Apple logo glowing brightly for all to see. The man next to me is listening to his iPod. Another customer has her Sony [VAIO]. The guy in the corner is displaying the Nike swoosh on his hat. Another fella has Hilfiger across his chest.

Fact is, we are a brand-loving society. Product placement is just a part of who we are and how we approach consumerism.

Jennifer A. Jones, "FCC to Crack Down on Product Placement," Speak Media Blog, June 24, 2008. www.speakmediablog.com.

In the early 1960s, Simkowski was advertising manager for Webcor, then a well-known brand of recording equipment made in Chicago.

"A guy at MGM [Metro-Goldwyn-Mayer, Inc.] called and said, 'We're making a movie with Bob Hope, and we need a Webcor tape recorder for a prop,'" Simkowski recalled.

"So I asked him, 'What's a prop?'—and then I made sure he got one."

Simkowski probably wouldn't have recognized the word "networking" back then, either, but he was already very good at it.

Invited onto the set of the Hope movie *Bachelor in Paradise*, he rubbed elbows with the star, who, he says, remembered him from a party both men had attended in 1953, when Simkowski was starting center on the first University of Wisconsin football team to play in the Rose Bowl.

That connection helped pave the way for a Webcor promotional campaign tied to the movie.

In 1980, still in Chicago but increasingly interested in the West Coast entertainment business, Simkowski founded Let's Go Hollywood Inc., a marketing agency that places clients' brand-name products in movies and TV shows.

The Budget rental truck in the 1990 movie *Home Alone?* That was his deal, Simkowski said. The Jim Beam whiskey in 1988's *Bull Durham*, 1993's *Groundhog Day* and the 1995 ice-fishing episode of *Frasier?* His, too.

Commercialism Is More Transparent in Television

In terms of product placement, TV and film have very different histories, Newell notes.

Taking their cue from radio, the companies that sponsored early TV shows placed their brand names right in the title. *Philco TV Playhouse*, *Texaco Star Theater* and *Kraft Television Theatre* were some of the most prestigious shows of the '50s.

Viewers who complain that *American Idol* has become one long Coke promotion, or that the *Queer Eye* guys lovingly reel off one brand name after another, may not realize that television's promotion of consumer products has never been confined to commercials.

[In February 2005], the U.S. Federal Trade Commission seemed to acknowledge that history when—in response to a request by Commercial Alert, an Oregon-based consumer advocacy group—it declined to require TV stations to disclose every instance of paid product placement to viewers.

Newell said that his Iowa State students not only don't object to product placement, they've come to expect it and to recognize it for what it is: one more way of saturating the atmosphere with commercial messages.

As for the effectiveness of those messages—well, that's another question.

Apple, Newell said, "has done an absolutely magnificent job" of placing its computers, with that unmistakable logo, in both feature films and TV shows, yet its market share remains tiny.

Then there's Bond. James Bond.

"If what we see in those movies really influences us to go out and buy the product," Newell asked, "shouldn't a lot more people be out there driving Aston Martins?"

Periodical Bibliography

The following articles have been selected to supplement the diverse views presented in this chapter.

Thomas Baggaley   "LDS Cinema Gets Better and Gets a Bum Rating," *Meridian Magazine*, February 20, 2004.

Peter Bart   "And Now, a Scene from Our Sponsors," *Daily Variety*, June 11, 2007.

William Booth   "Rating the Ratings," *Washington Post*, January 23, 2007.

Michael Boyer   "How Filmmakers Manipulate Movie Ratings," *World NetDaily*, October 21, 2008.

Christopher Campbell   "Rated BS: For . . . Broken System," *Cinematical*, January 18, 2007.

Gregg Cebrzynski   "Lights! Camera! Product Placement! Roles in Movies, TV Shows Give Chains Extra Brand Exposure," *Nation's Restaurant News*, December 4, 2006.

David M. Halbfinger   "Rating (and Finding) the Movie Raters," *New York Times*, January 16, 2006.

Anthony Kaufman   "Watching the Detectives," *Filmmaker*, Summer 2006.

David Loy   "Consciousness Commodified: The Attention-Deficit Society," *Tikkun*, July–August 2008.

Noel Murray and Scott Tobias   "Crosstalk: Does the MPAA Ratings Board Get a Bad Rap?" *A.V. Club*, June 22, 2007.

Andrew Salomon   "Product Placement: A Tangled Issue," *Back Stage East*, September 18, 2008.

What Is the Future
of the Film Industry?

Chapter Preface

On August 28, 2005, the *Washington Post* published an obituary—for the VHS (Video Home System) tape. During its twenty-nine years, the format "bravely won the war against Betamax and charmed millions of Americans by allowing them to enjoy mindless Hollywood entertainment without leaving their home. . . . It passed away peacefully after a long illness caused by chronic technological insignificance and a lack of director's commentary tracks." Major Hollywood studios began to phase out VHS releases in 2005. Bo Anderson, head of the Video Software Dealers Association, declared, "I would think 2006 is the last year that there are major releases on VHS, and there won't be many of those." In fact, national franchises such as Best Buy and Circuit City had stopped stocking such titles in the early 2000s.

What killed VHS exactly? The DVD—digital video disc—or digital versatile disc among technology enthusiasts. Development for the format began in 1993, led by Sony, Philips, Toshiba, and other electronics manufacturers. The DVD was first introduced in Japan in 1996, and in the United States in March of the following year. Its audio and video superiority and convenience made the DVD, which can be partitioned into easy-to-access chapters and sections, a success of blockbuster proportions, sending video rental stores and film buffs scrambling to replace their VHS libraries with the shiny, slim discs.

About ten years later, in 2006, the same companies that helped create DVD technology, Sony and Philips, unleashed its supposed successor, the Blu-ray Disc (which handily defeated Toshiba's obsolete HD-DVD), harkening the DVD's seemingly untimely end. The arrival of digital movie downloads also stokes predictions that hard formats will eventually be superseded. Meanwhile, VHS tapes have, indeed, largely disappeared. But they still fill the archives of television stations, and many movie aficionados have held on to their VHS players—not all movies have been re-released on DVD.

The rise and fall of technologies like the VHS tape shape the past, present, and future of the film industry. Authors in the following viewpoint discuss other issues and developments that have the potential to change, revolutionize, or even threaten, moviemaking.

> *"The lower the incidence of piracy, the less money studios would lose to film theft and the more they'd be able to invest in making, marketing, and distributing movies."*

Piracy Threatens the Future of the Film Industry

Annlee Ellingson

In the following viewpoint, Annlee Ellingson maintains that piracy is the film industry's biggest problem and that it results in economic repercussions on a global scale. Although the rate of piracy in the United States is 7 percent, the six major film studios that make up the Motion Picture Association of America (MPAA) lose billions of dollars a year due to DVD bootlegs and Internet downloads, Ellingson states. In addition, she claims that movie piracy has a domino effect that results in financial declines and job losses across the film industry, its partners, and suppliers. Ellingson is a former editor at Boxoffice, *a movie business magazine.*

As you read, consider the following questions:

1. What examples does the author provide to define what "piracy rate" means?

Annlee Ellingson, "The Piracy Problem: A 3-Part Series: Part 1," *Boxoffice*, vol. 143, 2007, pp. 39–45. © 2007 Boxoffice.com, LLC. All rights reserved. Reproduced by permission.

2. What figures does Ellingson provide for the number of jobs that would have been added to the U.S. economy without the effects of piracy?

3. According to Ellingson, why do people watch or buy pirated movies?

Hardly a day goes by that piracy isn't mentioned in the press, whether it's a report on the latest statistics on the effect of film theft on the industry, a description of some new initiative to combat it or an update on the latest pirate nabbed by authorities. Long overdue, however, is an in-depth examination of the problem. . . .

"The facts are pretty clear that this is a global problem with a significant economic impact," says Dan Glickman, chairman and CEO of the Motion Picture Association of America (MPAA). "A lot of countries lose tax revenue due to piracy. A lot of companies lose jobs as a result of this. And the fact of the matter is it's got a domino effect that affects people in other industries."

A Billion-Dollar Blight

According to a study prepared for the MPAA's global counterpart the Motion Picture Association (MPA) by LEK Consulting, members of the trade group, which are comprised of the six major film studios, lost $6.1 billion in 2005 to piracy worldwide. (Losses due to piracy were calculated based on the number of movie tickets and legitimate DVDs that consumers would have purchased had pirated goods not been available.) Eighty percent, or $4.8 billion, of these losses was due to piracy that occurred overseas, with 20 percent, or $1.3 billion, resulting from losses in the United States.

Abstractly these seem like big numbers. But a better question, perhaps, is the scale of the problem. LEK also measured piracy rates, assessing MPA member companies' revenue losses plus additional estimated losses in each market. China was the highest at 90 percent. That is to say, in China, 90 cents on every dollar that, absent film theft, would have been spent on movie tickets or DVD sales was lost to pirated goods instead. Russia and Thailand tied for second with 79 percent piracy rates each.

In the U.S., the piracy rate is seven percent. That may seem very low in the scheme of things, especially when compared to the rampant rates in China and Russia. But, if one considers that the 2005 domestic box office was $8.99 billion, at a piracy rate of seven percent, the industry lost $676.7 million in ticket sales. Without piracy, the box office could have reached $9.67 billion.

Likewise, consider piracy's effect on DVD sales. According to a separate MPA study, 1.1 billion DVDs were sold in 2005 at an average price of $21.35. That's $23.79 billion in DVD sales. Again, by applying the seven percent piracy rate, one finds that MPA member companies lost $1.79 billion in potential DVD sales, which without piracy could have totaled $25.58 billion.

The Distribution of Dollar Losses

Interestingly, worldwide it wasn't the countries with the highest piracy rates such as China where MPA member companies were hit hardest. Instead, in 2005 it was Mexico where dollar losses were highest with $483 million, followed by the United Kingdom and France.

This is because the U.S. motion picture industry's access to China is severely limited. In fact, the country allows only 20 foreign films to be shown on its screens each year. Operating outside the law, however, pirates can provide just about any and all American product.

"China is a special case because there is a quota on the number of our movies that can get in there," Glickman says. "But ironically you'll see virtually every movie that's ever been made on the streets of China. Movies that the censors in China will not let in the front door, they all are there [through] the back door. I'm talking about movies that are edgy, movies that are political, movies that are pornographic—it's all there."

When the impact of piracy is expanded to include not only the intellectual property owners—i.e., the distributors—but also the domestic and foreign producers, movie theaters, video stores and pay-per-view operators who also lose revenue to film theft, the LEK study found that losses increased almost threefold from $6.1 billion to $18.2 billion in 2005. In the U.S. losses all along the chain were $2.72 billion, while worldwide they totaled $15.46 billion. . . .

Organized Crime and Farmer John

Meanwhile, on the domestic front, a subsequent study found that the $6.1 billion that the MPA studios lost to piracy in 2005 grossly underestimates the total impact that film theft has on the overall economy. Using LEK's research as a starting point, a September 2006 analysis by the Institute for Policy Innovation (IPI) found that piracy not only results in lost revenue to motion picture businesses but also costs American workers both earnings and jobs and the government hundreds of millions of dollars in lost tax revenue to the tune of $20.5 billion in the U.S. alone.

While the LEK study estimated the losses experienced by the motion picture industry due to the global piracy epidemic, IPI's report takes an educated guess at the gains that would be experienced by U.S. industries, workers and governments if film theft were a non-issue. In other words, these are the damages sustained by the U.S. due to piracy, or, rather, the gains that could be realized if it were curtailed significantly.

Put it this way: The lower the incidence of piracy, the less money studios would lose to film theft and the more they'd be able to invest in making, marketing and distributing movies. More movies means more ticket sales at theaters and more popcorn sales at the concessions stand, which means more corn sales for the farmers who grow it, which means more seed and equipment sales for the dealers who sell them, and on down the line.

The Result of the Domino Effect

That's the theory, anyway. It's this entire retail chain that the IPI study examines. In economic terms, the greater the motion picture industry's output of product, the greater the output—i.e., sales of goods and services—of the businesses that supply the motion picture industry.

Applying these parameters using the RIMS II mathematical model, the IPI report estimates that American workers lose $5.5 billion due to piracy annually. Of this, $1.9 billion would have been earned by those working in the motion picture industry, whereas $3.6 billion would have been garnered by those working outside it. That's two-thirds of total lost earnings to U.S. workers due to piracy affecting those who don't even work in the motion picture or retail industries.

Moreover, the study found that, without the effects of piracy, 141,030 jobs would have been added to the U.S. economy. Of these, 46,597 would have been in the motion picture industry; 94,433 outside it. Again, two-thirds of lost U.S. employment due to piracy occurs in industries outside motion picture production and retail.

Finally, IPI's analysis concluded that piracy costs the U.S. government at all levels $837 million in lost tax revenue. Of this, an additional $147 million in corporate income taxes from motion picture companies could have been collected had piracy not been a factor, $91 million from motion picture production or sales; and $599 million in personal income taxes that would have been paid to federal, state and local governments.

The Seeds of Discontent

Given these startling statistics, piracy clearly is a significant problem facing the movie industry. There are myriad reasons for its steep rise.

For some, DVD bootlegs or Internet downloads (which account for 62 percent and 38 percent of piracy, respectively, according to LEK's report) are the only way to acquire some pieces of entertainment content. For example, one 26-year-old graduate student downloads movies or TV shows "usually because they're not available any other way—i.e., the original videodisk version of the *Star Wars* trilogy . . . was just released on DVD [recently]," she says. "Occasionally something is only available to purchase, not to rent. I may steal in that case, too."

"The unavailability often of legitimate product at reasonable prices that is available easily is one issue that a lot of people have raised," agrees Glickman of the MPAA.

The unavailability of content is perhaps an even larger issue overseas. There's the case of China, of course, where the government strictly restricts the availability of theatrical and home-video products. But piracy is a threat anywhere where a movie's not showing when it's available somewhere else.

"Clearly we hear that a lot," Glickman says. "If the [difference between the] release [date] in the U.S. and release [date] overseas is extensive, then you offer an opportunity for people to offer the stuff on the street. That may account for some piracy that's there."

Others argue that movie tickets are too expensive. This is among the reasons two urban teens, dubbed Spike and Blacksheep, buy bootleg DVDs.

"It's a money thing," says Spike. "I never go to the movies."

Bootlegs and Internet Downloads
Are Cheap and Easy

"They're cheap. I can't afford theater tickets. Bootlegs come to you," adds Blacksheep, referring to the distributors who approach hangouts with suitcases of illicitly copied DVDs for purchase. "I usually don't go to the movies either. Maybe once every couple of months. But, if the prices were lower, I would go to more movies because I like seeing movies at the theater."

"When we've done our own surveys of why people like or don't like movies, why they go or don't go to movies, or why they steal or don't steal, sometimes generically they will talk about things in the movie experience they don't like, for example the cost or the environment they may not find as attractive," admits Glickman.

But mostly the appeal of acquiring pirated goods is that it's cheap or free and easy. One 25-year-old grad student, who says he doesn't do it so much anymore, would download movies from the Internet as an undergrad because "the wonders of a 'free' T3 connection made it easy and fun." LEK found that 44 percent of MPA company losses in the U.S. are attributable to college students.

"I'd say the biggest thing is convenience," the student continues. "Downloading is so easy, and it's free. I hate to encourage American laziness, but, when something is free and easy, it's very difficult to turn down."

Glickman finds this reasoning perhaps the most pervasive. "By and large the reasons are pretty much the same," he says. "When you can get stuff for virtually free on the street [or on the Internet], an awful lot of people will take advantage of it. People have always wanted to copy what other people have done and not pay for it. The difference now is with digital transmission it's a lot easier to do it, it's a lot faster to do it, and it's a lot harder to catch."

Indeed, with advances in computer technology, piracy— both the production of DVD bootlegs and the dissemination of content via the Web—is easier, faster and cheaper than ever before. "The ease of copying material and using digital distribution techniques to ship material around the world makes it a far more threatening problem than it would have been just dealing with pirated DVDs on the street," Glickman says.

The Industry Fights Back

The challenge for the studios, then—both individually and through their trade organization the MPAA—is to make the illicit acquisition of their content more difficult and expensive for consumers to acquire. There's no one approach, however, that will get the job done.

"I think it was H.L. Mencken who said, 'For every complicated problem, there is a simple and a wrong solution,'" Glickman says.

Keeping that sage advice in mind, the MPAA and its member studios have initiated a multi-front attack on piracy. Strategies include legislation and litigation, law enforcement, education, preventive measures and out-of-the-box tactics that double as publicity stunts to further draw public attention to the problem. . . .

To combat film theft, the first weapon in the MPAA's arsenal is legislation, followed up by litigation. "We need good laws in countries around the world and strong enforcement of those laws, especially against those who are engaging in massive, illegal pirate operations," says Vicki Solmon, senior VP of trade regulation and copyright protection in Sony's legal division.

"In the U.S.," adds the MPAA's Glickman, "we've been working to pass laws both at the state and federal levels which deal with camcording, which deal with prerelease of movies that aren't out yet [and which deal] with piracy and theft on the Internet generally. And we've enforced those criminally and civilly inside the United States."

Signed by President [George W.] Bush in 2005, the Family Entertainment and Copyright Act renders camcording a movie off a cinema screen a federal offense and criminalizes the theft of content that has not yet seen commercial release. In addition, 39 states have established laws against the use of recording devices in theaters, with penalties ranging from high misdemeanors to felonies.

Most recently, these efforts paid off with the successful prosecution of Johnny Ray Gasca, a Hollywood man who was caught camcording in private screenings of *The Core*, *8 Mile* and *Anger Management*. The first person to be charged in a federal crackdown on piracy, Gasca was convicted of three counts of copyright infringement and sentenced to 84 months in federal prison. . . .

Out-of-the-Box Strategies

Recently the MPA added two new members to its global anti-piracy team: a pair of black Labrador Retrievers named Lucky and Flo. Much like dogs have been taught to sniff out bombs and uncover trapped humans, the Irish-born canines trained for eight months to detect the polycarbonate and other chemicals used in optical disks. Lucky and Flo are unable to distinguish between legitimate and illicit products, but, because legal shipments are usually registered on shipping manifests, the dogs' skills will still be useful in locating disks shipped in unlikely or unregistered containers.

Another line of defense is education. "We need to make sure that the public understands that piracy is illegal and it is harmful to the economy." Sony's Solmon says. "We want people to know that if they buy or download a pirated movie, they are very likely to get an inferior quality product—nothing like the magical experience of seeing a great movie like *Casino Royale* on a big screen with an enthusiastic audience around them. And, in many cases, consumers of pirated products simply get ripped off entirely with a disk of something completely unrelated to what they thought they were buying or a file on their computer that is either empty or unwatchable."

"We do a lot of publicity to try to let people know that [piracy] is wrong, that it has a harmful impact economically, it costs jobs, it costs revenue, that it's illegal," Glickman says. "Our job is to try to make it so that people know they can't hide, and, if they do get caught, they will pay and face consequences."

During the [2006] holiday season, the MPAA, in collaboration with its Recording Industry counterpart, launched a "Holiday Blitz" PR [public relations] campaign designed to alert holiday shoppers to signs of piracy in their media gift purchases. The promotion included tips for consumers such as "You get what you pay for" and "Too new to be true."

The main target for the MPAA's educational efforts, however, are young people. "A big part of piracy really starts with kids—kids in high school, even younger," Glickman says. "You see a lot of intellectual property infringement on college campuses as well."

Strategies include withholding the location of exhibitor screenings and veiling the title of the picture being screened at the venue; employing private security at research, press and premiere screenings, including, for advance public showings of *Spider-Man 2* in Latin America, helicopter surveillance; and shipping prints in three or four parts, with the reels arriving in random order.

Such measures pay off, Solmon says. "No copies of two of our biggest global releases [in 2007] *The Da Vinci Code* and *Casino Royale*, were found on the Internet or on pirate DVDs prior to their international theatrical release."

Finally, perhaps the most effective preventive measure is to offer consumers content in the convenient forms they prefer. "The most creative thing that's happening now is that there is a rapid development of new ways to get entertainment material to consumers—faster, more convenient and reasonably priced—using the modern digital transmission methods," Glickman says. "Most people don't want to break the law. . . . In the same way that the movie industry has responded over the years by making the picture better, the sound better, the quality better, we're also now participating in getting the material to consumers in the way they want to read it, look at it, watch it."

*"While the reports have succeeded in at-
tracting considerable attention, a closer
examination of the [film] industry's
own data reveals that the claims are
based primarily on fiction rather than
fact."*

The Piracy Threat to the Film Industry Has Been Exaggerated

Michael Geist

*In the following viewpoint, Michael Geist insists that the film
industry's claims of financial loss due to piracy are inconsistent
and unsubstantiated. For instance, Geist alleges that the reported
rates of camcorder piracy—including figures from a lobby group
that includes the Motion Picture Association of America
(MPAA)—differ wildly and have not been subjected to an independent audit or review. He also contends that both Canadian
and U.S. lobby groups portray Canada as a "piracy haven" despite lauding the nation's anti-piracy measures. Geist is the
Canada Research Chair of Internet and E-commerce Law at the
University of Ottawa, Canada.*

Michael Geist, "Hollywood Claims of Movie Piracy More Fiction than Fact," *Ottawa Citizen*, February 6, 2007. Reproduced by author's permission.

As you read, consider the following questions:

1. What Canadian percentages of global camcording does Geist provide?

2. Why are the financial harms of camcorder piracy exaggerated, in Geist's opinion?

3. According to the author, why have revenues from movie theaters shrunk?

In [early 2007], Canadians have been subjected to a steady stream of reports asserting that Canada has become the world's leading source of movie piracy. Pointing to the prevalence of illegal camcording—a practice that involves videotaping a movie directly off the screen in a theatre and transferring the copy on to DVDs for commercial sale—the major Hollywood studios are threatening to delay the Canadian distribution of their top movies.

While the reports have succeeded in attracting considerable attention, a closer examination of the industry's own data reveals that the claims are based primarily on fiction rather than fact.

In the best Hollywood tradition, Canadians have been treated to a show from the Motion Picture Association of America (MPAA) and its Canadian counterpart (the Canadian Motion Pictures Distributors Association [CMPDA]) that is much ado about nothing, featuring unsubstantiated and inconsistent claims about camcording, exaggerations about its economic harm and misleading critiques of Canadian law.

The Camcorder Claims

First, the camcorder claims have themselves involved wildly different figures. [In January and February 2007], reports have pegged the Canadian percentage of global camcording at either 40 or 50 per cent. Yet the International Intellectual Property Alliance, a U.S. lobby group that includes the MPAA, ad-

Colleges Are Singled Out Unfairly

In its campaign urging lawmakers and colleges to take the issue of on-campus illegal file sharing seriously, the Motion Picture Association of America has wielded an array of legal arguments, facts and statistics. . . .

The association often notes that according to a 2005 study it commissioned, 44 percent of the money the industry lost within the United States that year was attributable to peer-to-peer file sharing by college students. It now appears that the figure was closer to 15 percent.

Andy Guess, "Downloading by Students Overstated,"
Inside Higher Ed, *January 23, 2008. www.insidehighered.com.*

vised the U.S. government in late September [2006] that Canadians were the source for 23 per cent of camcorded copies of DVDs.

Not surprisingly, none of these figures has been subject to independent audit or review. In fact, AT&T Labs, which conducted the last major public study on movie piracy in 2003, concluded that 77 per cent of pirated movies actually originate from industry insiders and advance screener copies provided to movie reviewers.

Moreover, the industry's numbers indicate that camcorded versions of DVDs strike only a fraction of the movies that are released each year. As of August 2006, the MPAA documented 179 camcorded movies as the source for infringing DVDs since 2004.

During that time, its members released about 1,400 movies, suggesting that approximately one in every 10 movies is camcorded and sold as infringing DVDs. According to this data, Canadian sources are therefore responsible for camcorded DVD versions of about 3 per cent of all MPAA member movies.

Second, the claims of economic harm associated with camcorded movies have been grossly exaggerated. The industry has suggested that of recently released movies on DVD, 90 per cent can be sourced to camcording.

The Real Financial Impact

This data is misleading not only because a small fraction of recently released movies is actually available on DVD, but also because the window of availability of the camcorded versions is very short. Counterfeiters invariably seek to improve the quality of their DVDs by dropping the camcorder versions as soon as the studios begin production of authentic DVDs (which provide the source for perfect copies).

Camcorded DVDs, which typically feature awful sound and picture quality, ultimately compete with theatrical releases for only a few weeks and likely have very limited impact as they do not represent a viable substitute for the overwhelming majority of moviegoers.

In fact, as the movie industry has grown—global revenues have nearly tripled over the past 25 years—the importance of theatre revenues has shrunk. In 1980, theatre box office revenues represented 55 per cent of movie revenue. Today, DVDs and television licensing capture the lion share of revenue, with the box office only responsible for approximately 15 per cent of movie revenue.

In other words, the economic impact of camcorded DVDs—which involve only one in 10 releases and impact a small part of the revenue cycle—is little more than a rounding error in a $45 billion (U.S.) industry.

Third, claims that Canadian copyright law is ill-equipped to deal with camcorder piracy are similarly misleading. Canadian law already renders it illegal to make for sale or rental an infringing copy of a copyrighted work such as a movie. The Copyright Act includes severe penalties for violating this provision with the potential for million dollar fines and up to five years in jail.

A Frightening Finale

Indeed, the MPAA's own Web site specifically points to Canada as an example of how many countries have laws that prohibit illegal camcording. The movie lobby states, "in Canada camcording is an infringement under the Copyright Act, regardless of whether it is for the public or personal use of the person making the copy."

Moreover, the CMPDA's Web site trumpets dozens of arrests for DVD and movie piracy in Canada. Over [2006], the RCMP [Royal Canadian Mounted Police] and local police forces laid charges for DVD piracy on numerous occasions, while a Canadian court upheld a U.S. decision to fine a Canadian operator nearly $500,000 (Canadian) for copyright infringement related to movie piracy.

As for claims that tough U.S. laws are pushing camcording into Canada, the president of the U.S. National Association of Theatre Owners told his members in November that illegal camcording in the U.S. has expanded [from 2005 to 2007] from New York and Los Angeles to at least 15 states.

Despite all the evidence to the contrary, the U.S. and Canadian lobby groups continue to portray Canada as a piracy haven while pressing for unnecessary legal reforms. Unless politicians separate fact from fiction, this show appears headed for a frightening finale.

"... it's astounding to see how much it has changed the way movies are made, the stories they tell, where they're shown, how much they cost, and who's watching."

Digital Movies Are the Future of the Film Industry

Steven Ascher

Steven Ascher is an Academy Award nominated director whose films include Troublesome Creek *(winner of Sundance Grand Jury Prize) and* So Much So Fast. *He is author of* The Filmmaker's Handbook, a Comprehensive Guide for the Digital Age, *a bestselling text. In the following viewpoint, Ascher claims that the digital era is transforming how motion pictures are made, distributed, and seen. For example, the author maintains that digital video technology is reducing production costs, thus allowing filmmakers to bypass major studios and inexpensively produce and distribute movies through the Internet to specialized audiences. Ascher further contends that from digital projectors to high-definition televisions to tiny MP3 player screens, movies are reaching audiences in many new ways.*

Steven Ascher, "The Digital Revolution," eJournalUSA, June 2007. Reproduced by permission of author.

As you read, consider the following questions:

1. In Ascher's view, how did digital technology initially change the film industry?
2. In the author's opinion, why was *The Blair Witch Project* a huge success?
3. According to Ascher, what is filmmaker George Lucas's view of the future of movie theaters?

In the history of motion pictures there have been decisive moments when a new technology changed everything. In 1927 *The Jazz Singer*—the first "talkie"—marked the beginning of the sound era. Suddenly, as comically portrayed in *Singin' in the Rain*, silent film stars were out and a new type of star and a new type of story were in, changing how movies were written, filmed and shown.

Today, digital technology is driving a revolution that's even more earthshaking. Children who have grown up in the Internet era don't realize how seismic the changes have been. Movies—all kinds of media, really—will never be the same.

What digital means technically is that pictures and sounds are converted to digital data (ones and zeros) that can be stored, manipulated and transmitted by computers. Once in digital form, a world of possibilities opens up.

The digital era in movies began in the 1980s, but picked up momentum around 1990. From the beginning, digital technology was used to create new kinds of images. George Lucas's company, Industrial Light and Magic pioneered astonishing visual effects that made the most fantastic space stories look stunningly realistic. With programs like Photoshop we could now digitally alter pictures—say, to remove a person or add a building—which changed our basic understanding of photographed reality. In the digital era, statements like "pictures don't lie" and "seeing is believing" are clearly untrue. Digital editing systems helped shape new filmmaking styles and techniques, such as the use of very short shots, graphics that fly around the screen and objects that seamlessly transform (morph) into other objects. The look of most TV commercials today would not be possible without digital tools.

The 1990s brought an explosion in digital video (DV) and the now-familiar miniDV camcorders that give amateurs the ability to shoot and edit inexpensive, very good-quality video. Independent filmmakers seized DV cameras and used them to make movies that were suddenly being shown on television and at prestigious film festivals like Sundance. In the traditional Hollywood production model, films are shot with big 35mm film cameras with big crews to handle them. While DV is not up to 35mm quality, it's good enough and cheap enough that a wide range of fiction and documentary projects can be made in DV that would have been impossible, or impossibly expensive, before.

As digital video took off, so did the Web. At first, Hollywood didn't know what to do with it. *The Blair Witch Project*, a 1999 low-budget thriller shot with small-format video cameras, is credited as the first movie to exploit the Internet's marketing power. By posting hints on the Web that the horror in the film was real, the producers sparked intense debate, helping propel the film to a $248 million worldwide gross. Today, Web sites, blogs, online reviews and discussions on sites like MySpace.com are essential elements in building "buzz" for a new film.

The Web opens the door to a new model of filmmaking and distribution. The majority of movies are created and distributed by large corporations—such as film studios, television broadcasters or big distribution companies. However, the Web makes it possible to produce a movie for a specialized audience and sell DVDs (yet another digital technology) directly to that audience, bypassing the gatekeepers who would have likely rejected the project for lack of broad appeal. Distribution expert, Peter Broderick notes that *Reversal*, a drama about high school wrestling, has never been shown in the-

The Art of Digital Production

There is a powerful recycling effect in Hollywood—as digital techniques for rendering textures such as hair, water and fire are pioneered in films such as *Stuart Little* and *The Perfect Storm*, they become part of movieland's collective effects arsenal, eventually being packaged in software such as Autodesk Maya Hair and Maya Fur. Elements and tools—from digital characters and environments to motion-capture techniques that record actors' movements and facial expressions—now are handled routinely, with confidence rather than crossed fingers. Stefen Fangmeier, an alum of George Lucas's Industrial Light & Magic (ILM), sounds matter-of-fact as he discusses the elaborate work he and his crew have done on his directorial debut, an adventure fantasy called *Eragon*. "Is there a tremendous amount of new technology in this? No," Fangmeier says. "It's the way we're putting it together and applying it to this character. A dragon has never been done like this."

Tom Russo, *"Movies 2.0: Digital Effects Magic Explained,"* Popular Mechanics, *January 2007. www.popularmechanics.com.*

aters, on TV or even offered in video stores, but has generated over a million dollars in sales of DVDs and merchandising over the Web. *In The Long Tail: Why the Future of Business is Selling Less of More,* author Chris Anderson describes how the Web enables producers and distributors to target niche audiences with products that don't sell in high enough volume for traditional retail outlets. The ability to make a profit while producing smaller and more unusual types of productions increases as we move away from selling or renting physical objects like DVDs and toward downloading electronic files.

Meanwhile, recent advances in high definition television (HDTV) have brought a quantum leap forward in picture and sound quality. If you've been to an electronics store lately, you know how incredibly clear, vivid and downright huge the new flat-panel screens are. Every frame of digital video is made up of tiny dots of light called pixels; the more pixels, the sharper and better the image, especially when shown on a big screen. Traditional, standard definition video uses about 345,000 pixels for each frame; the best high definition systems use about two million. Once you've seen a beautifully shot, widescreen movie in high definition, you never want to go back to watching old-fashioned standard def again.

High definition is transforming Hollywood movies and TV shows (using camera technology pioneered by, once again, George Lucas). Many types of projects that used to be shot on film are now shot in high definition to save time and money; the quality is now high enough that audiences usually can't tell the difference. Almost every movie today goes through a digital stage at some point in its production.

The Digital Cinema Initiative was put forth by a group of studios to bring digital technology all the way to theaters. Currently, when you go to your local multiplex, chances are you're watching a movie being shown with a film projector. New "4K" digital projectors use almost nine million pixels and create a gorgeous picture that never gets scratched or dirty. Theaters have resisted investing in the expensive machines, but because studios can save millions by not having to manufacture and ship heavy film prints, they may eventually subsidize the equipment. However, Hollywood is terrified of the potential for piracy when their new releases come out in digital form. Piracy is already an enormous problem. When the latest James Bond film opened recently in foreign theaters, the pirated DVD was already available on the street.

But just as theaters are poised to move into the digital era, consumers have an exploding number of options for viewing movies on giant flat-panel screen in their living rooms, on smaller computer screens at their desks, and on tiny iPod or cellphone screens on the street. Digital television—already available with new high definition and standard definition channels—will completely replace traditional analog TV in the United States on February 17, 2009. Between video-on-demand, downloads, TiVO, and Webcasts, we'll soon be able to see almost anything, anywhere, anytime. Will this mean the death of one of the great worldwide traditions—going to a theater to watch a movie surrounded by an audience that's laughing and crying along with you?

Yet again, we look to George Lucas as a bellwether. Because releasing a movie theatrically is incredibly risky and expensive, studios are driven to a blockbuster mentality, creating product for the widest possible appeal (or, depending on how you see it, the lowest common denominator). Even so, most films lose money in the theaters. Lucas, the man behind more blockbusters than almost anyone, told *Daily Variety*, "We don't want to make movies. We're about to get into television." Instead of spending $100 million to make a single film and another $100 million to distribute it to theaters, he said, he could make fifty to sixty films for TV and Internet distribution. As for future audiences going to theaters, Lucas said, "I don't think that's going to be a habit anymore."

When you consider that digital technology is at its heart simply a way to convert movies to a string of ones and zeroes, it's astounding to see how much it has changed the way movies are made, the stories they tell, where they're shown, how much they cost, and who's watching. Stand by for further developments.

> *"Big chains like AMC and Regal Enter-*
> *tainment are all grasping for a Holy*
> *Grail—a way to remake moviegoing*
> *into what it once was: an experience*
> *unlike any other."*

Movie Theaters Are Adapting to Changes in the Film Industry

Andy Serwer

Andy Serwer is the managing editor of Fortune *magazine and a noted business journalist. In the following viewpoint, Serwer claims that, in order to remain relevant amidst the home enter-tainment boom, the American movie theater is undergoing a radical transformation. He states that movie theater chains are in the stages of going "premium," making way for martini bars, screen-side services, and super-crisp digital screens. According to Serwer's forecast, the moviegoing experience of the future will encompass the fine details of a big night out for the family—the steakhouse dinner and kids' chaperone included.*

As you read, consider the following questions:

1. As stated by the author, how has movie attendance changed since the 1940s?

Andy Serwer, "Movie Theaters: Extreme Makeover," *Fortune*, May 23, 2006. © 2006 Time Inc. All Rights Reserved. Reproduced by permission.

2. According to Serwer, what happened in the movie theater business in the 1990s?

3. What are the benefits of digital screens for movie theaters, in Serwer's view?

Shari Redstone is holding court in the lobby of a movie theater in Millbury, [Massachusetts], rattling on in her usual Gatling-gun staccato.

The daughter of 82-year-old supermogul Sumner Redstone and president of National Amusements—the family-owned theater business that also holds controlling stakes in Viacom and CBS—she's proudly showing off one of her company's newest emporiums, when all of a sudden she stops cold and points.

"Look," she says in a Boston accent that would make Cliff from *Cheers* proud, "it's ahr mah-tini bahr!" And though it's just past noon, Redstone insists we go in and sample the merchandise. After a belt or two I mention that this might not be a bad place to frequent on a Friday night, which of course is exactly what she wants to hear.

Cocktails are just one facet of Redstone's meta-strategy to transform moviegoing into what she calls "premium" entertainment. She has also dreamed up "chocolate bahs," screen-side waiter service, and high-end food. She's already showing live broadcasts of baseball games—make that Red Sawx games—with kids walking up and down the aisles hawking peanuts. Meanwhile, other operators are renting out theaters to *Fortune* 500 companies for meetings or even to churches for religious services.

It's all part of a mad scramble by theater owners to keep their venues relevant (and full) in our increasingly digital age.

"It's an interesting time to be in the movie theater business," says CEO [chief executive officer] Steve Marcus of Marcus Theatres, a 500-theater chain out of Milwaukee. "But I don't sleep as well as I used to."

A Glorious History

For much of their 100-year history, movie theaters were the exclusive venue for Hollywood to exhibit its glittery wares. In the heyday of moviegoing, which stretched from the grand urban palaces of the 1920s through the quintessential 1950s drive-in, theaters were the ultimate escapist destination. For less than a buck you were swept into another world (replete with air conditioning, buttery popcorn, and if you were lucky, a date) that the phonograph or radio couldn't come close to approximating.

Back in 1946, buttressed by the appeal of newsreels, movie theaters sold some four billion tickets in the U.S., at a time when the total population was 141 million. That's 28 movies a year, on average, for each and every American.

But in the 1950s television began to gnaw away at movies' stranglehold on entertainment, and by 1973 ticket sales fell to 864 million. While attendance has climbed since—to 1.4 billion tickets [in 2005]—it still pales in comparison with old times. With the U.S. population now around 300 million, the average American goes to the movies less than five times a year.

The simple fact is that today theaters are less singular than they have ever been. The business is under assault from so many fronts that exhibitors (as theater owners are called) almost don't know whom to shoot back at: home-theater sellers like Best Buy, black-market distributors of pirated films, on-line movie downloaders, movie studios that spit out cookie-cutter sequels while shortening the wait for DVD releases, and of course endless new forms of digital entertainment, from iPods to YouTube to video games.

While some operators continue to thrive—buoyed by ever-rising ticket prices and profitable concessions—there is no way a smelly, threadbare theater with scratchy sound can survive in this environment.

Remaking Moviegoing

Redstone, with her cocktail lounges and other coming attractions, and her cohorts at the other big chains like AMC and Regal Entertainment are all grasping for a Holy Grail—a way to remake moviegoing into what it once was: an experience unlike any other. Redstone, 51, remembers when she first described the concept of a newfangled, high-end movie theater to her father.

"He was asking me these questions, and I knew he just didn't get it. Finally I said to him, 'Look, do me a favor and don't even talk to me about it until I finish one.' Then he saw one and phoned me right away and told me, 'I get it.'"

What Shari Redstone is referring to is what she calls a Cinema De Lux (or CDL) theater. National Amusements now has 11 of them in the U.S., and Redstone says she ultimately plans to convert half of her 1,000 or so domestic venues.

The 14-screen CDL megaplex in Millbury (just south of Worcester) where I met Redstone looks at first glance like any other suburban-mall theater. But starting with the martini bar—a concept Redstone conceived while on vacation in the Maldives (towns like Millbury aren't exactly bursting with martini bars)—and moving into the center lobby, where a baby grand piano sits next to a virtual soccer game for kids, you begin to think otherwise.

Along with traditional concessions, there's a mini Ben & Jerry's and a Starbucks. There's a lounge with comfy couches and end tables stacked with newspapers and magazines. A concierge desk assists patrons who need a taxi or help purchasing tickets. The theater also houses two private-function rooms that are available for birthday-party rentals and other events.

And then there are the theaters themselves. Two are what Redstone calls "director's halls," fitted with Ultra Leather rocking recliners, reserved seating for all performances, live intros before showings, and escorted seating service. In some CDL theaters, liquor may eventually be served screen-side. (Talk about the Holy Grail!)

"We are trying our hardest to get people out of the house to see a movie," Redstone says. "We simply must give people an experience they can't get elsewhere."

Yes, the theater business survived the body blow of television, but what sort of shape is it in today?

Doomsayers suggest the business is in an irreversible decline and point to the fact that ticket sales have skidded three years in a row—a slump that hasn't happened since the '50s. Defenders say the business has been taking punches for decades from new competitors like HBO, DVDs, and home theaters, and will continue to motor along. This most recent decline, they say, is just another cyclical downturn due to poor product (can you say *Bewitched* and *The Island?*), and in fact, [in 2006] through May 9 the box office is up 5.4 percent.

"It's unlikely there's a permanent downward decline," asserts Mike Savner, an analyst with Bank of America Securities. "International box offices were far worse than the U.S. [the past few years], which is important," he explains, "because the penetration rates outside the U.S. for Internet, video games, and home theater systems are all significantly lower than in the U.S. So [bad] product has the most to do with it."

The Good Times

It's hard to imagine that at one time movie theaters were so lucrative the feds had to step in and break the party up. When the movie business started a century ago, studios quickly realized they were ignoring a valuable profit center by letting other entrepreneurs exhibit their films.

The solution was pursuing vertical integration, and by the 1940s the Big Five studios controlled most of the country's theaters. The government sued on antitrust grounds, and in 1948 the Supreme Court ruling in *United States v. Paramount Pictures* forced the studios to divest.

Drive-Ins Reclaim a Solid Niche

Once teetering on the brink of extinction, drive-ins have made a modest recovery, with many of the surviving theaters enjoying their biggest success in years. It's unlikely we'll ever see another boom in drive-in construction, as we did between the end of World War II and the Watergate era, but drive-ins seem to have found a solid niche by appealing to retro-pop enthusiasts—and by reminding us of what made them so fun in the first place.

Once we've allowed nostalgia to steer us to the nearest drive-in, where we unload the folding chairs, fire up the hibachi and pull a PBR [Pabst Blue Ribbon] out of the cooler, we realize what a singular experience it was—and still is—in this age of indoor malls, arena rock shows and enclosed sports venues. It's a place where you can be surrounded by a sellout crowd, but it doesn't feel crowded because you're in your own cocoon. You can walk around, chat with friends or go get some Goobers without missing any of the action. And if someone drags her screaming kids to the movies, as long as they're locked in the car, that's her problem, not yours.

Scott Henry, "Drive-in Revival," Creative Loafing, *June 26, 2002.*

The single-screen downtown theater, which dominated the business for 30 years, eventually gave way to the suburban multiplex, which in 1995 begat the first standalone megaplex. Located in Dallas, AMC's Grand 24 (screens) wasn't attached to a mall but instead was designed as a destination unto itself. It was extremely successful—yet as it turned out, that sowed the seeds for yet another disastrous era in showing movies.

"We had such a terrific run for much of the 1990s," recalls Redstone. "The movies were great, attendance was up, and it began to attract financial players. Developers were building like crazy, and they would tell you if you didn't put a theater in their complex, they would find someone else, which drove up rents. So not only did the business become overbuilt, but many operators had economic models that couldn't work."

And the Bad Times

From 1990 to 1999, the number of movie screens in the U.S. rocketed up 57 percent, to more than 37,000. Yet the number of tickets sold climbed only 20 percent.

That disparity caused the industry to go splat, with six major chains, including Regal, Carmike, and United Artists, filing for bankruptcy as the century turned. Some 2,000 screens were soon shuttered. Balance sheets were eventually shored up in a wave of consolidation that has seen some 12,000 screens change hands [from 2002 to 2006] alone.

Did the crash of 2000 spell the end of the megaplex? No, though the newest giants, like Redstone's CDLs, could be called postplexes because of all their new features. Size still matters, says David Brain, CEO of Entertainment Properties Trust, a REIT [Real Estate Investment Trust] that develops theaters.

"It's really not that different from the retail category, creating selection at a single location," he says. "That's why Americans shop large-format retailers, and we are conforming to that."

In those 18- to 24-screen complexes, multiple theaters show hot new releases to give the convenience of varying starting times.

"It's the same reason that you go to Linens 'n Things for towels," says Brain. "You get every color, every size, every weight. You get what you want when you want it."

Like Redstone, Brain sees exhibitors stepping up concessions, a model that works especially well when you're serving 4,000 to 6,000 people a day, which is what those complexes are bringing in.

Developers are beginning to look at locating theaters in tandem with restaurants, bowling alleys, and skating rinks too. Exhibitors are experimenting with live events: Regal movie theaters are used by churches in Washington, D.C., Houston, Orlando, and Buford, [Georgia]. (This reportedly has led to some confusion by younger parishioners, who sometimes believe they are about to see a Sunday-morning screening of *Madagascar*.) Regal and others have also leased theaters to companies like Microsoft, Sprint, eBay, and American Express for corporate events, complete with big-screen satellite presentations.

Digital Improvement

The full optimization of theaters will come, experts say, when the business converts from celluloid to digital. The new format will allow not only for instant and dirt-cheap distribution of films but also for targeted distribution of independent films, distinct versions for unique audiences, subtitles, and dubbing, never mind beamed-in rock concerts or kids' shows.

"Digital is a very big deal," says Dan Fellman, president of domestic distribution at Warner Bros. "It's going to take some time, but it could save our industry billions of dollars."

The only problem: The cost savings that Fellman refers to—print and shipping expenses, which would be unnecessary in a digital world in which a film is simply downloaded—fall to distributors. Yet exhibitors have to shell out for the digital projectors, which cost more than $100,000 per screen.

Wall Street financier Ronald Perelman, for one, who owns the film-equipment company Panavision, is betting the transition to digital will go slowly. In January [2006] he bought film-service company Deluxe for $750 million.

"Deluxe can transition to digital services along with the rest of the business," says Perelman. "When that happens, I don't have a clue. Right now it's not even clear what the savings would be if you really drill down."

[In 1999] *Fortune* ran a piece about the movie business going digital: "Both studios and exhibitors say they expect that digital distribution should begin in three to five years and that it will be widespread by next decade's end." In that year, 1999, there were ten digital screens in the U.S.; today there are [more than 5,000].

Adoption is going somewhat better with online ticketing, which Redstone says now accounts for up to 8 percent of her theaters' seats. Such ticketing is dominated by two players: Movietickets.com (owned by a group of media companies and theater chains, including National Amusements, Marcus, and AMC) and the larger Fandango (founded by a rival group of theater owners, including Regal and Carmike, and a couple of venture capital firms).

What about a merger between Fandango and Movietickets, so moviegoers have a one-stop shop?

"My guess is that something would happen eventually," says AOL [America Online] chief Jon Miller. (Movietickets is the back-end processor for AOL's Moviefone.) "[Consumers] would know where to get movie tickets," Miller goes on, "and that would help adoption in online ticketing happen faster."

Redstone says that there have been discussions between the two e-ticketers, but that "cultural" differences remain.

A Glimpse at the Future

Consider, then, the movie experience of the future. Earlier in the week you ordered and printed your tickets online from a single Web site (accumulating points for a free vacation). Of course you picked your favorite seats, 12D and 12E. On Saturday a taxi ordered by the theater picks up you and the family at 6 p.m. sharp and whisks you to a steakhouse in the theater complex.

At 7:45 a theater sitter takes the kids to either the chaperoned game zone or a PG-rated feature, while you stroll over to your own R-rated film. You are met by an usher who seats you in a plush swivel chair and takes your afterdinner drink order. The lights dim, and the super-crisp digital print appears on the screen.

Afterward there is the nightcap at the mahtini bahr. Then you pick up the kids and head home via theater cab. If that sounds as if it's worth leaving the house for, theater owners may live to fight for another hundred years. If not . . .

> *"With box-office attendance sliding . . . many in the industry are starting to ask . . . whether it reflects a much bigger change in the way Americans look to be entertained—a change that will pose serious new challenges to Hollywood."*

Home Entertainment Technologies Decrease Movie Attendance

Laura M. Holson

In the following viewpoint, Laura M. Holson claims that the habits of American moviegoers are changing: more people are opting to stay in with pay-per-view, DVDs, and video games. She suggests that box-office attendance is slumping because technological leaps in home entertainment have given viewers more to watch or play at their convenience on large, high-definition flat screens in surround sound, no less. In order to recapture their core audience, the author recommends that movie studios reinvigorate their role in generating excitement. Holson is an award-winning reporter for the New York Times *and former writer for* Money *magazine.*

As you read, consider the following questions:

1. According to the author, how have Americans' video- and DVD-watching habits changed between 2000 and 2004?
2. How have the sales and marketing of DVDs changed, in Holson's view?
3. What reasons does Holson provide to support her view that home entertainment theaters are keeping moviegoers at home?

Matthew Khalil goes to the movies about once a month, down from five or six times just a few years ago. Mr. Khalil, a senior at the University of California, Los Angeles, prefers instead to watch old movies and canceled television shows on DVD.

He also spends about 10 hours a week with friends playing the video game *Halo 2*. And he has to study, which means hours on the Internet and reading at least a book a week.

"If I want to watch a movie I can just rent it on DVD," he said. "I want to do things that conform to my time frame, not someone else's."

Like Mr. Khalil, many Americans are changing how they watch movies—especially young people, the most avid moviegoers. For 13 weekends in a row, box-office receipts have been down compared with [2004], despite the blockbuster opening of the final *Star Wars* movie. And movie executives are unsure whether the trend will end over the important Memorial Day weekend that officially begins the summer season.

Meanwhile, sales of DVDs and other types of new media continue to surge.

With box-office attendance sliding, so far, for the third consecutive year, many in the industry are starting to ask whether the slump is just part of a cyclical swing driven mostly by a crop of weak movies or whether it reflects a much bigger change in the way Americans look to be entertained—a change that will pose serious new challenges to Hollywood.

A Cultural Shift

Studios have made more on DVD sales and licensing products than on theatrical releases for some time. Now, technologies like TiVo and video-on-demand are keeping even more people at home, as are advanced home entertainment centers, with their high-definition television images on large flat screens and multichannel sound systems.

"It is much more chilling if there is a cultural shift in people staying away from movies," said Paul Dergarabedian, president of the Exhibitor Relations Company, a box-office tracking firm. "Quality is a fixable problem."

But even if the quality of movies can be improved, Mr. Dergarabedian said, the fundamental problem is that "today's audience is a much tougher crowd to excite. They have so many entertainment options and they have gotten used to getting everything on demand."

[In 2004] Americans spent an average of 78 hours watching videos and DVDs, a 53 percent increase since 2000, according to a study by the Motion Picture Association of America [MPAA], the film industry's trade group. DVD sales and rentals soared 676.5 percent during the same period, and 60 percent of all homes with a television set now also have a DVD player. DVD sales and rentals alone were about $21 billion, according to the Digital Entertainment Group.

Discs are now released just four months after a film's debut, and the barrage of advertising that accompanies the opening in movie theaters serves ultimately as a marketing campaign for the DVD, where the studios tend to make most of their profits.

Dissatisfaction with the Moviegoing Experience

The global decline in movie theater attendance ... reflects a dissatisfaction with the moviegoing experience and increasing competition for the consumer's share of time and money, this according to a global survey of consumers conducted by PA Consulting Group and the Motion Picture Association of America. ...

For example, 86% of all respondents stated that they would attend a movie at a theater if ticket prices were reduced substantially. Furthermore, 62% of all respondents indicated that they would be more likely to attend a movie if they had the option of reserved seating.

PRNewswire, *"Movie Attendance Linked to Theater Experience, Increased Competition for Consumer Time, According to PA Consulting Group Survey,"* January 4, 2007. www.prnewswire.com.

By contrast, movie attendance has increased 8.1 percent from 2000 to 2004, according to the association. Many in the movie industry point to that figure as a sign of overall health. But attendance was down in three of those five years, and the sharp increase in attendance in 2002 is attributed to the overwhelming success of *Spider-Man* and *Star Wars: Attack of the Clones.*

More recently, the number of moviegoers has dropped, sliding 4 percent in 2003, 2 percent in 2004 and 8 percent so far in 2005.

Time spent on the Internet has soared 76.6 percent and video game playing has increased 20.3 percent, according to the association. [In 2004], consumers bought $6.2 billion worth of video game software, an increase of 8 percent from

2003, according to the [global market research company] NPD Group, which tracks video game sales.

This does not mean that the $9.5 billion theatrical movie business is anywhere near its last gasp. It still plays a crucial role for the studios in generating excitement. But movie makers recognize they have to be more on their toes if they want to recapture their core audience.

Distractions from the Movie Theaters

"There are a lot of distractions," said Jerry Bruckheimer, who produced *Pirates of the Caribbean* in 2003 as well as the successful *CSI* television franchise. "You need to pull them away from their computers. You need to pull them away from their video games."

Consider Matt Cohler, a 28-year-old vice president at Thefacebook.com, a Silicon Valley company that creates Internet student directories on college campuses. Mr. Cohler likes movies, but lately, he said, little has grabbed his attention.

He liked the new *Star Wars* and a documentary about the collapse of Enron. But of the Nicole Kidman-Sean Penn big-budget thriller, *The Interpreter*, Mr. Cohler said, "It was only O.K." He has few plans to see anything else this summer [2005], and said he was content to spend his free time online or writing e-mail.

"I feel quite strongly that, with a few exceptions, the quality of movies has been declining the last few years," he said.

Amy Pascal, the chairwoman of Sony Pictures Entertainment's motion picture group, said, "We can give ourselves every excuse for people not showing up—change in population, the demographic, sequels, this and that—but people just want good movies."

She predicted that *Bewitched*, a romantic comedy about a producer who unwittingly hires a "real" witch for the lead role in a remake of the television show, would have a broad appeal. "If it was a straight-ahead remake of the show," she said, "we would have been guilty of doing the ordinary."

Jill Nightingale, 37, who works at IGN Entertainment in ad sales, is the type of moviegoer—older, female and important to studios—that *Bewitched* should appeal to. But video games increasingly have taken up time she otherwise might spend watching television or going to the movies. The last two theater showings she said she attended were *Star Wars* and *Sideways*, which she viewed in December [2004].

She plays a video game for 30 minutes each night before bed. [In May 2005], five friends joined her at her San Francisco condo to drink wine and play *Karaoke Revolutions* on her Sony PlayStation, where the would-be American Idols had a competition, belting out everything from Top 40 hits to show tunes.

"Party games are great for dates," she said. "A few years ago I would have been at a bar or at a movie."

The Greatest Impact

But what could well have the greatest impact on theater attendance is the growing interest in digital home entertainment centers, which deliver something much closer to a movie-style experience than conventional television sets.

Brian Goble, 37, a video game entrepreneur, said he had not been to a movie theater in two years, except to see *Star Wars* with his wife and four friends. Instead, he stays at his home in a Seattle suburb, where he has turned the basement into a home theater with a 53-inch high-definition television screen and large surround-sound speakers. He no longer has to deal with parking and jostling crowds, he said, a relief now that he has two children.

"It's really just not as comfortable and fun as being at home," he said. "You can pause, go to the bathroom, deal with a crying kid."

Mr. Goble rarely watches video-on-demand ("The quality is poor," he said.) Instead he has an account with Netflix and orders his movies online. When the Nicolas Cage movie *National Treasure* was released [November 2004], for instance, he added it to his Netflix list so he would be sent a copy when it came out on DVD.

His prime regret about seeing the final installment of *Star Wars* was that he could not watch it at home. "The only reason to go to the theater these days," he said, "is because it is a movie you must see now."

> *"Movies have been a refuge for the cash-strapped—as a place to forget about everyday troubles and a way to stretch tight household budgets."*

Movie Attendance Increases During Recessions

David Germain

David Germain is a movie writer for the Associated Press. *Germain states in the following viewpoint that when a recession hits, Americans head to the movies. Drawing upon historical claims, the author maintains that ever since the Great Depression of the 1930s, movie attendance has been robust during economic slumps. And, according to Germain, even though television and other forms of entertainment may have taken a toll on box-office attendance throughout the decades, the lure of movies as a temporary escape is especially powerful when budgets are tight.*

As you read, consider the following questions:

1. What examples does Germain provide to support his claim that Hollywood is "recession-proof"?

David Germain, "When Consumers Yell 'Cut!' Hollywood Thrives," *Associated Press*, March 10, 2008. Reproduced by permission.

2. According to Germain, what events and activities are more expensive than a movie ticket?
3. During the 1930s, what was shown at movie theaters, as stated by the author?

Hollywood thrives when the economy dives.

It was true during the Depression, when Americans scraped together nickels and dimes for an escape to the movies. And as the prospect of another recession looms, studio executives say this time is no different.

As evidence mounts that people are tightening up on other expenses, movie attendance [in 2008] has been running ahead of 2007 numbers—welcome news at ShoWest, the annual convention of theater owners that opens [March 10, 2008].

Domestic box-office revenue went up in five of the past seven recession years dating to the 1960s, according to research compiled by the National Association of Theatre Owners. While budget-conscious consumers in today's economic downturn may hold off buying that 50-inch plasma television, "it seems they can always pull together the money to go to the movies," film historian and critic Leonard Maltin said. "They're not making a monthly commitment or a down payment. They're just shelling out the 10 bucks."

Holding Its Own

Economists are still debating whether the U.S. economy is headed for recession—or already in one—but closely watched indicators have been bleak, with employers shedding jobs and consumers reeling from high gas prices and tight credit.

Meanwhile, Hollywood is more than holding its own, with revenue running 4 percent ahead of [2007's], according to box-office tracker Media By Numbers.

Factoring in higher admission prices, attendance was up 7 percent over last year as of [March 2008], before the arrival of a few box-office duds, including the Will Ferrell comedy *Semi Pro*. Attendance has since fallen back to a gain of 0.5 percent.

Though virtually everyone gripes about the cost of snacks at concession stands, the average movie ticket price [in 2007] was $6.88—cheaper than sporting events, concerts or a night out bowling.

"Most people would believe that offers a very good value. It's certainly much cheaper than a psychiatrist," said Dan Glickman, who heads the Motion Picture Association of America, Hollywood's top trade group. "To go into a darkened room where nobody can find you for two hours is great therapy, particularly when times are bad."

Since the Depression of the 1930s, when a quarter or less could buy a full day's entertainment at a theater, movies have been a refuge for the cash-strapped—as a place to forget about everyday troubles and a way to stretch tight household budgets.

"We don't want to wish recession on anyone or hard times on anyone, but we certainly have done very well during recessions," said John Fithian, president of the theater owners group, who planned to touch on Hollywood's recession-proof history in a speech at ShoWest's opening. Amid America's longest and bleakest economic bust in the 1930s, movie attendance tumbled initially as investment money for films dried up. But in the heart of the Depression from the early to late 1930s, attendance shot up.

History Repeats Itself

While detailed box-office figures were not released back then as they are today, as many as 4.6 billion movie tickets a year were sold in the 1930s—three times more than in 2002, the best year of modern times. And the U.S. population during the Depression was less than half of today's 300 million.

Granted, there was simply less to do then.

Economic Pullbacks Signal Increased Movie Attendance

- In 1974 and 1975, as the economy contracted 0.5% and 0.2%, respectively, after 5.8% growth in 1973, the annual box-office take rose 25% and 11% as Americans sought refuge from reality in hits like *Jaws, The Towering Inferno* and *Blazing Saddles*. Movie-theater attendance rose 16.9% in 1974 and 2.2% in 1975.

- In 1982, the economy contracted 1.9%, after 2.5% growth in 1981. Box-office takes shot up 16.4% as hits such as *E.T.: The Extra-Terrestrial* and *Porky's* offered escapes. The number of moviegoers was up 10%.

- In 2001, economic growth slowed to 0.8% from 2000's 2.7%, but box-office spending on movies such as *Monsters, Inc., The Mummy Returns* and *Ocean's Eleven* rose 9%. This was also the year the *Harry Potter* and *Lord of the Rings* film franchises were launched. Then, the box-office take rose 14% in 2002 as economic weakness lingered, growing only 1.6%. Movie-theater attendance went up 4% in 2001 and 11% in 2002.

Michael Brush, "Indiana Jones vs. the Recession,"
MSN Money, *April 9, 2008. http://articles.moneycentral.msn.com.*

"What were your options? Radio, books and movies," said Paul Dergarabedian, president of Media By Numbers. "You didn't have the iPod. You had your Victrola. We didn't have video games. We had, I don't know . . . tiddlywinks."

In those days, projectors ran virtually nonstop as feature films were accompanied by cartoons, newsreels and short films. Much of the schedule was devoted to glossy musicals, slapstick and screwball comedies that took people's minds off the gloomy economy, from Marx brothers comedies such as *A Night at the Opera* to Fred Astaire and Ginger Rogers dancing cheek to cheek in *Top Hat.*

"When the economy gets a little bit sluggish, our business seems to do well or even pick up," said Dan Fellman, head of distribution for Warner Bros., which is trotting out key celebrities at ShoWest such as George Lucas, Steve Carell and Christian Bale to plug its summer lineup, which includes *Star Wars: Clone Wars*, *Get Smart*, *Speed Racer* and the Batman sequel *The Dark Knight.*

Fellman, whose father worked in theaters starting in 1928, said movie houses have survived all new competition for people's entertainment time and money—from radio during the Depression, television in the 1950s and home video in the 1980s.

The Chance to Get Away

Television did take a calamitous toll on movie theaters, whose audiences steadily declined through the mid-1970s to less than a fourth of their numbers in the late 1940s. Attendance generally was flat into the early 1990s but has improved since then as theaters with better seating, sound and concessions became the standard.

Besides the possible looming recession, there are other factors drawing more people to the movies: Fans can buy tickets online so they can avoid turning up for sold-out shows. And recent hits such as *Hannah Montana & Miley Cyrus Best of Both Worlds Concert* demonstrate the mass appeal of movies shown in the three-dimensional digital format.

But for all the technological improvements, the basic lure of movies is the same as it was in the Depression—the chance to get away. And that may be especially powerful in a time when economic woes are heavy on Americans' minds.

"It's escape from everything," Maltin said. "It's a chance to, like all those song lyrics, 'forget your troubles, come on get happy.'"

Periodical Bibliography

The following articles have been selected to supplement the diverse views presented in this chapter.

Jen Chaney	"Parting Words For VHS Tapes, Soon to Be Gone With the Rewind," *Washington Post*, August 28, 2005.
Cineaste	"Film Criticism in the Age of the Internet," Fall 2008.
Kenneth C. Green	"The Movie Industry's 200% Error," *Inside Higher Ed*, January 29, 2008.
Kate Greene	"Preventing Movie Piracy," *Technology Review*, July 5, 2006.
Michael Greeson	"Movie Downloads: Why This Model Won't Work," *Billboard*, April 22, 2006.
Andy Guess	"Downloading by Students Overstated," *Inside Higher Ed*, January 23, 2008.
Daniel Harris and Don Tuite	"Video Processing Brings New Meaning to Motion," *Electronic Design*, September 1, 2006.
Nazir Keshvani	"Financing the Independent Film," *Asia Image*, September 2006.
Scott Kirshner	"Studios' Digital Dilemma," *Variety*, November 2, 2007.
Josh Levin	"AXXo You Are a God: The Secrets of Bit Torrent's Top Movie Pirate," *Slate*, November 12, 2008.
Jonathan Parkyn	"Convert VHS to DVD," *Computer Act!ve*, February 16, 2006.

For Further Discussion

Chapter 1

1. David Thomson argues that violent movies have potentially negative impacts on young viewers. However, Gordon Dahl and Stefano DellaVigna maintain that violent movies decrease violent crime because they attract potential perpetrators to theaters. In your opinion, who makes the more compelling argument? Use examples from the viewpoints to develop your answer.

2. Do you agree with David Goldenberg's argument that audiences are not influenced by movies to engage in at-risk behavior? Why or why not?

3. Joe R. Feagin claims that Hollywood movies portray white identity and institutions positively, even in settings of extreme racism. Michael E. Ross focuses on the achievements and widening recognition of minorities in Hollywood. In your opinion, which is more important to racial equality? Explain your answer.

4. Nathan Gardels and Mike Medavoy contend that foreign countries associate Hollywood blockbusters with a violent, permissive, and materialistic culture. What are some of the values promoted in the internationally produced Hollywood movies that Hans Erik Næss discusses?

Chapter 2

1. The Motion Picture Association of America responds to the question of how its raters determine the rating category of a movie in its viewpoint. Does the association's explanation help you understand its ratings system better? Use examples from the viewpoints to explain your response.

2. Steve Persall and Steven D. Greydanus disagree on whether or not movie ratings have become more lenient. Do the authors share any of the same views? Explain your answer.

Chapter 3

1. Jesse Walker maintains that Frederic Howe and Jack Valenti played contradictory roles because they aided censorship through self-regulation. Do you agree or disagree with the author? Use examples from the viewpoints to develop your answer.

2. Joanne Weintraub suggests that some critics romanticize early Hollywood as being free of commercialism. In your opinion, does Robin Good romanticize early Hollywood in his viewpoint? Why or why not?

Chapter 4

1. Michael Geist states that the piracy statistics used by the Motion Picture Association of America and other organizations are inconsistent. Does Annlee Ellingson use data that is consistent in her argument against movie piracy? Use examples from the viewpoints to explain your response.

2. Andy Serwer reports that movie theaters are transforming themselves to compete with home entertainment. In your opinion, will premium services and new amenities attract moviegoers? Why or why not?

3. David Germain claims that box-office attendance rises during economic downturns. Does the author successfully address the issue of high prices at movie theater concession stands? Explain your answer.

Organizations to Contact

The editors have compiled the following list of organizations concerned with the issues debated in this book. The descriptions are derived from materials provided by the organizations. All have publications or information available for interested readers. The list was compiled on the date of publication of the present volume; the information provided here may change. Be aware that many organizations take several weeks or longer to respond to inquiries, so allow as much time as possible.

Academy of Motion Picture Arts and Sciences
8949 Wilshire Boulevard, Beverly Hills, CA   90211
(310) 247-3000
Web site: www.oscars.org

The Academy of Motion Picture Arts and Sciences, a professional honorary organization of over 6,000 motion picture professionals, was founded to advance the arts and sciences of motion pictures; foster cooperation among creative leaders for cultural, educational and technological progress; recognize outstanding achievements; represent the viewpoint of actual creators of the motion picture; and foster educational activities between the professional community and the general public. It sponsors the Academy Awards, or Oscars, every February.

Amateur Movie Makers Association (AMMA)
Web site: www.ammaweb.org

Amateur Movie Makers Association (AMMA) is a nonprofit educational organization devoted to promoting interest among its members and the public in the art and craft of amateur moviemaking in all formats. It is also a forum for getting ideas and help from some of the best amateur film and video makers in the United States and Canada. It publishes a monthly newsletter, *The Monitor*.

The Film-Makers' Cooperative

108 Leonard Street, 13th Floor, New York, NY 10013
(212) 267-5665 • fax: (212) 267-5666
e-mail: film6000@aol.com
Web site: www.film-makerscoop.com

The Film-Makers' Cooperative is the largest archive and distributor of independent and avant-garde films in the world. Created by artists in 1962, as the distribution branch of the New American Cinema Group, the Film-Makers' Cooperative has more than 5,000 films, videotapes, and DVDs in its collection.

Motion Picture Association of America (MPAA)

1600 Eye Street, NW, Washington, DC 20006
(202) 293-1966 • fax: (202) 296-7410
Web site: www.mpaa.org

Founded in 1922, the Motion Picture Association of America (MPAA) and its international counterpart the Motion Picture Association (MPA) serve as the voice and advocate of the American motion picture, home video and television industries.

National Association of Movie Theatres (NATO)

750 First Street NE, Suite 1130, Washington, DC 20002
(202) 962-0054 • fax: (202) 962-0370
e-mail: nato@natodc.com
Web site: www.natoonline.org

The National Association of Theatre Owners (NATO) is the largest exhibition trade organization in the world, representing more than 29,000 movie screens in all fifty states, and additional cinemas in fifty countries worldwide. Its membership includes the largest cinema chains in the world and hundreds of independent theatre owners.

National Film Board of Canada (NFB)

PO Box 6100, Montreal, Quebec   H3C 3H5
  Canada
(800) 267-7710 • fax (514) 283-7564
Web site: www3.nfb.ca

The National Film Board of Canada (NFB) is Canada's public film producer and distributor of documentary films, auteur animation, alternative drama, and more. It has been involved in over 12,000 productions and received more than 5,000 awards, including twelve Academy Awards.

National Institute on Media and the Family

606 Twenty-Fourth Avenue South, Suite 606
Minneapolis, MN   55454
(888) 672-5437 • fax (612) 672-4113
Web site: www.mediafamily.org

The National Institute on Media and the Family seeks to educate and inform the public and to encourage practices and policies that promote positive change in the production and use of mass media. It does not advocate censorship of any kind. It aims to partner with parents and other caregivers, organizations, and corporations to create media choices for families.

Screen Actors Guild (SAG)

5757 Wilshire Boulevard, 7th Floor
Los Angeles, CA   90036-3600
(323) 954-1600
Web site: www.sag.org

Established in 1933, the Screen Actors Guild (SAG) exists to enhance actors' working conditions, compensation and benefits and advocate artists' rights. With twenty branches nationwide, SAG represents nearly 120,000 actors who work in motion pictures, television, commercials, industrials, video games, Internet, and all new media formats.

Sundance Institute
PO Box 684429, Park City, UT 84068
(435) 658-3456 • fax: (435) 658-3457
e-mail: institute@sundance.org
Web site: www.sundance.org

Sundance Institute is a nonprofit organization dedicated to the discovery and development of independent artists and audiences. Through its programs, the institute seeks to discover, support, and inspire independent film and theatre artists from the United States and around the world, and to introduce audiences to their work. It sponsors the annual Sundance Film Festival.

Bibliography of Books

Charles R. Acland — *Screen Traffic: Movies, Multiplexes, and Global Culture.* Durham, NC: Duke University Press, 2003.

George Alexander — *Why We Make Movies: Black Filmmakers Talk About the Magic of Cinema.* New York: Harlem Moon, 2003.

Richard Barrios — *Screened Out: Playing Gay in Hollywood from Edison to Stonewall.* New York: Routledge, 2003.

Peter Bart — *Boffo!: How I Learned to Love the Blockbuster and Fear the Bomb.* New York: Hyperion, 2006.

Peter Biskind — *Down and Dirty Pictures: Miramax, Sundance, and the Rise of Independent Film.* New York: Simon & Schuster, 2004.

Francis G. Couvares — *Movie Censorship and American Culture.* Amherst, MA: University of Massachusetts Press, 2006.

Arthur De Vany — *Hollywood Economics: How Extreme Uncertainty Shapes the Film Industry.* New York: Routledge, 2004.

Thomas Doherty — *Hollywood's Censor: Joseph I. Breen and the Production Code Administration.* New York: Columbia University Press, 2007.

Jack C. Ellis and Betsy A. McLane — *A New History of Documentary Film.* New York: Continuum, 2005.

Edward Jay Epstein — *The Big Picture: The New Logic of Money and Power in Hollywood.* New York: Random House, 2005.

Mark Harris — *Pictures at a Revolution: Five Movies and the Birth of New Hollywood.* New York: Penguin Press, 2008.

Bell Hooks — *Reel to Real: Race, Sex, and Class at the Movies.* New York: Routledge, 2008.

Scott Kirshner — *Inventing the Movies: Hollywood's Epic Battle Between Innovation and the Status Quo, from Thomas Edison to Steve Jobs.* CinemaTech Books, 2008.

Spencer Lewerenz and Barbara Nicolosi, eds. — *Behind the Screen: Hollywood Insiders on Faith, Film, and Culture.* Grand Rapids, MI: Baker Books, 2005.

Toby Miller, Nitin Govil, John McMurria, Ting Wang, and Richard Maxwell — *Global Hollywood No. 2.* London, UK: British Film Institute, 2008.

Colin Odell and Michelle Le Blanc — *Horror Films.* London, UK: Oldcastle Books, 2008.

James Robert Parish — *Fiasco: A History of Hollywood's Iconic Flops.* Hoboken, NJ: Wiley, 2008.

Kendall R. Phillips — *Projected Fears: Horror Films and American Culture.* Westport, CT: Praeger Publishers, 2005.

| William H. Phillips | *Film: An Introduction (Fourth Edition)*. New York: Bedford/St. Martin's Press, 2009. |

David Rensin — *The Mailroom: Hollywood History from the Bottom Up*. New York: Ballantine Books, 2003.

Jim Taylor, Mark R. Johnson, and Charles G. Crawford — *DVD Demystified (Third Edition)*, New York: McGraw-Hill, 2006.

Jack Valenti — *This Time, This Place: My Life in War, the White House, and Hollywood*. New York: Harmony Books, 2007.

Stephen Vaughn — *Freedom and Entertainment: Rating the Movies in an Age of New Media*. New York: Cambridge University Press, 2006.

David Waterman — *Hollywood's Road to Riches*. Cambridge, MA: Harvard University Press, 2005.

Jessica Winter — *The Rough Guide to Independent Film*. New York: Rough Guides, 2006.

Lauren Witter-Keller and Raymond J. Haberski Jr. — *The Miracle Case: Film Censorship and the Supreme Court*. Lawrence, KS: University of Kansas Press, 2008.

Index